THE
Gettysburg
Diaries

*War Journals of Two
American Adversaries*

THE
Gettysburg
Diaries

*War Journals of Two
American Adversaries*

Mark Nesbitt

GRAMERCY BOOKS
NEW YORK

Previously published as *35 Days to Gettysburg*

This 2008 edition is published by Gramercy Books, an imprint of Random House Value Publishing, by arrangement with Stackpole Books. Originally published by Stackpole Books under the title *35 Days to Gettysburg.*

Gramercy is a registered trademark and the colophon is a trademark of Random House, Inc.

Random House
New York • Toronto • London • Sydney • Auckland
www.valuebooks.com

A catalog record for this title is available from the Library of Congress.

ISBN: 978-0-517-23078-7

Printed and bound in the United States.

10 9 8 7 6 5 4 3 2 1

For my mother, Ethel,
who taught me to be gentle enough to write

And for my father, Burton,
who taught me to be tough enough to be a writer

Acknowledgments

W riting is supposed to be a very lonely occupation. I have never found it to be so. Everything I've written for publication has been a cooperative effort, with individuals happy to share their knowledge and their valuable time to help.

And while the kindness and generosity of these people is remarkable, my memory is not. This book has taken a number of years to compile and write. I have attempted to keep track of all those who have helped me in even the smallest way, and yet I know there are some I met on Virginia back roads who gave me valuable information, whose names I have forgotten. If you remember helping and are not listed here, my sincerest apologies. Your help was appreciated, if not here acknowledged.

First I must recognize the Southern Historical Collection at the University of North Carolina, Chapel Hill, for the use of the Gettysburg segment of the Thomas Lewis Ware Diary. In particular I must thank Dr. Richard Shrader, whose cooperation in this project was vital. I wish also to recognize the efforts of the late Cmdr. Robert L. Brake, who spent much of his spare time in libraries around the country gleaning bits and pieces of historical trivia associated with the Battle of Gettysburg and sending them to Gettysburg National Military Park and the U.S. Army Military History Institute, Carlisle Barracks, Pennsylvania. It was from Commander Brake's work that I first heard of Thomas Lewis Ware. Dr. Richard J. Sommers, Archivist-Historian of the U.S. Army Military History Institute was, as always, very helpful in my original search for appropriate diaries.

Mr. Lawrence Eckert, Curator of Collections, Gettysburg National Military Park, allowed me access to the Franklin Horner

Diaries and gave permission to use the Gettysburg segments. His help was important and greatly appreciated.

Corresponding with Mary W. Probst, grandniece of Thomas Ware, was one of the more delightful experiences I've had in researching. To know someone who was that close to a historical individual reminded me that the Civil War was not all that long ago. Mary provided priceless, unpublished information on the Thomas Ware family and made Thomas and Robert Ware real people instead of merely names. I hope she is pleased with the results of our work.

Kenneth L. Norman, who is related to the Normans mentioned by Thomas Ware in his diary, is another whose love for family heritage and the truth about Southern history is enormous. He has carefully researched and collected the details of the Ware-Norman family connections and acted as my liaison with Mary Probst and Lincoln County, Georgia. He provided the background for much of the biographical segments throughout this work.

My research in Culpeper County, Virginia, was aided by Rosemarie Martin, who graciously invited me to her home and introduced me to Mr. J. Russell Guinn. Both helped me to familiarize myself with the area about which Thomas Ware spent a good bit of his time writing.

Edward G. J. Richter has done an impressive amount of work (which is truly never ending) on the burial sites of soldiers on the battlefield of Gettysburg and their subsequent removal. If it weren't for his research I might not have located on the battlefield specific original burial sites.

Herbert O. Brown, author and co-proprietor of *Fields of Glory* in Gettysburg, did the legwork in Savannah and photographed the probable final resting place of Thomas Ware.

Dr. Richard H. McCormick and his daughter, my longtime friend Linda McCormick, donated their time to locate and photograph the grave of Franklin Horner. Joan Bossmann and Barbara Wickerham, two other close friends, shared their knowledge and hospitality with me while I was on the road researching.

Some professional historians were involved in this project as well, and I am indebted to them for their solid advice and encouragement: Greg Coco, Kathy Georg-Harrison, Tracy Bearden, and Robert Prosperi for his reading of the manuscript.

A good bit of my research was done by automobile. I found it impossible to juggle modern maps and the massive *Atlas to the Official Records*, read Thomas Ware's or Franklin Horner's diary entries and look for details that they mentioned, and still stay on the road. My research assistants not only helped me piece together the routes Thomas Ware and Franklin Horner followed to Gettysburg, but probably saved my life a number of times. My thanks for that go out to Ellen Abrahamson, Martha Good, Cheri Kershner, Kate Roulette, Tracy Stivers, and Danette Taylor.

And finally, I thank the people with the never-ending patience, my editors at Stackpole Books, Mary Suggs and Ann Wagoner.

Most of the people who helped me did so for the cost of lunch, or the film required to take photos, or a few beers. I'm certain that meager remuneration was not their purpose for helping. Instead, they helped because of their love for history and a desire to share their specialized knowledge with those who appreciate it. The unselfishness of the people I've met while researching the American Civil War is virtually universal and remains one of the warmest memories of the several years of work involved in this book. I thank them all with heartfelt admiration.

*"… men of near blood born,
made nearer by blood shed."*

—Major General Joshua L. Chamberlain

The collision course, June 1–July 2, 1863

○ ○ ○ *Ware's route*   ● ● ● *Horner's route*

Introduction

If the American Civil War began as a great celebration, it ended as one unbelievable funeral procession. Of the more than three million soldiers involved, a horrifying 20 percent died.[1] It made all our previous wars seem like minor skirmishes in scope, and it would forever make Americans kin to the rest of the war-filled world. We went off to the war—the two sections—as joyous celebrants; we came back from it a single nation of corpses or mourners. Many of us mourn still.

To most Southerners, the coming war represented their happy bid for independence, seen by many of them early in the war as the same type of divine struggle that was fought against Great Britain four score and five years before. To them, the beginning of the war was like the new Fourth of July. There were speeches and firecrackers and flags, celebrating the creation of a brand new country that was all their own and separate from an oppressive, tyrannical overlord. No more would the politicians from the North meddle in their affairs of society and property. They would have freedom and their rights.

For many in the North, it seemed a glorious test of whether the United States was indeed "a more perfect Union" as the forefathers had intended or merely a loose hodgepodge of individual commonwealths temporarily thrown together by revolutionary necessity and maintained by geographical accident. To those north of Mason's and Dixon's line, victory would ensure that the

---

[1] Livermore. Exact figures are virtually impossible to ascertain since many Confederate records were destroyed in the flight from Richmond at the end of the war. For a while when Grant took over the Union Army, the casualties were so high they ceased reporting them since, according to Joshua Chamberlain, "the nation would not stand it if they knew."

Fourth of July, the great holiday of freedom, would continue to be celebrated for the same reasons it always had—for "life, liberty and the pursuit of happiness" in a country where "all men are created equal."

Both sides, then, were fighting for freedom.

If anyone on either side had bothered to remember their history, they would have realized that American independence did not come without cost: 4,435 killed in battles over eight years of warfare in the Revolution against Mother England.[2] If anyone thought they knew what price would have to be paid for going to war in a new revolution, they would have found themselves grossly underestimating the cost in American lives, fortunes, and social trauma.

The suddenness of war made the young men and women of both sides giddy with excitement. Young men rushed to enlist as their friends had, so that the war would not end before they had an opportunity to "see the elephant." Young women, in spite of Victorian reserve, became overnight brides when their rough school suitors turned up as uniformed men with polished buttons.

The coming of war was, at last, a change from the boredom of farm life in the South and small-town-clerk life in the North. The bold adventure of battle was covered with the glory of following the flag into the fray and living to tell the stay-at-homes about it. And if they fell, they would fall nobly, gracefully, floating, they imagined, wrapped in the folds of the nation's banner. It would be a painless, dreamlike sacrifice. Whatever happened, they would come home heroes.

But once the men marched off, the celebrations stopped. The party ended with the last strains of "Good Night, Ladies." The next day began far too near sunrise with the raspy bugle call to drill.

Certainly the newspapers of both sections headlined great victories early in the war to a believing public. But the newspapermen—like the homebodies—had not been in the battles yet, or through the tedium of daily drill, or the helpless horror as thousands of men died of the mysterious and seemingly incurable ailments

---

[2] Johnson, 308.

known as "camp fever," or measles, or even diarrhea. Soon the believing public lost faith in great victories as the personal emotional convulsion of suddenly having a dead soldier in the family instead of a live brother or son or husband was felt. Soon the stories of glory simply would not fit into the newspapers because of the growing length of the casualty lists.[3]

The names of thousands of small, never-heard-of but never-to-be-forgotten streams, and creeks, and -burgs, and -villes, and mountains, and rivers, and ridges, and country churches, and railroad junctions were staining the American consciousness blood-red forever. In 1861: Fort Sumter, Big Bethel, Manassas, Wilson's Creek, Balls Bluff. 1862: Fort Donelson, Pea Ridge, Shiloh, New Orleans, Seven Pines to Malvern Hill, Cedar Mountain, Manassas again, Antietam, Corinth, Perryville, Fredericksburg, Stone's River. 1863: Port Hudson, Chancellorsville, Vicksburg. Then, after twenty-six months of indecisive warfare: Gettysburg. The Gettysburg campaign changed the course of the war and altered the lives of hundreds of thousands of individuals, including two particular American soldiers, Thomas Ware and Franklin Horner.

The American Civil War was fought by writers. Thousands of the participants kept—or tried to keep—daily entries in small pocket diaries and journals. These diaries, often leather-bound, were just the right size to fit in a waistcoat pocket. Many of them were originally published blank except for dates and printed lines for entries. Today they are frail, faded, and prone to crumbling into dust in your hand. They've been through a great deal.

Perhaps not so surprisingly, most of a soldier's life in the army did not find him in battle, but rather in the mundane tasks of camp life such as cooking, washing, drilling, cleaning weapons, and more drilling. He usually had more than enough time, even after writing one or two letters to family and friends, to spend five minutes jotting down in his pocket diary the events, both momentous and seemingly insignificant, of that particular day. Reading these daily entries, one can almost feel the dew on the fence rail the soldier used as a writing desk or smell the sour canvas of his damp dog tent.

---

[3] Johnson, 308. In just the Union armies alone, the casualty rates, excluding captured and missing, were 29.2 percent. Confederate casualties were probably higher.

These unpublished diaries, of which literally hundreds are extant, are truly fascinating when combined with details of the campaigns and battles that the men write about. The soldiers did not write with you or me or posterity in mind, nor did they have the training of an educated historian or the prescience of a seer; they never thought that anyone, except a few family members or close friends, would ever read their words, so their view is somewhat narrow. They rely on camp rumor for "facts" regarding the war; they don't have access to maps to tell them where they are or where they are headed on the march; and they certainly have neither the hindsight nor the foresight to inject their entries with anything but what they perceive as the simple truth.

The common soldiers' diaries are certainly not great works of literature. When these soldiers attempted to become literary, they nearly always failed. But there is something special, something vital and immediate in their terse, often ungrammatical sentences. These men wrote because they could—often barely so—or because they were bored, or because their friends did, or perhaps because they felt a small stirring within that this personal experience of civil war they were witness to would someday be important. They probably never thought that their own experiences would ever be of interest to anyone but themselves.

Several years ago it was my good fortune, while doing research for another project, to have the opportunity to scour the archives of some of the country's most prestigious repositories of first-person accounts of experiences in the American Civil War. I visited the National Archives, the Library of Congress, the Gettysburg National Military Park collection of diaries, and the U.S. Army Research Institute at Carlisle, Pennsylvania, and telephoned and wrote to a dozen more archival institutions. I perused more than three hundred diaries and collections of letters, both published and unpublished.

From those collections I gleaned half a dozen accounts that seemed to fit my criteria: young soldiers, on the Gettysburg Campaign, with lucid, direct, written impressions of their lives as soldiers.

The thought of tracing the march routes of two American enemies on a collision course and finding them, after a month-long odyssey, within musket range of each other was always in the back of my mind. The odds of finding two such diaries are slim. But as I studied the accounts, I realized that two of the diaries chronicled the daily experiences and marches that pulled their authors into the whirlpool of combat on virtually the same battlefield at Gettysburg.

The daily diary entries of Thomas Lewis Ware, a Confederate soldier from rural Georgia, and Franklin Horner, a Union soldier from the coal country of Pennsylvania, are presented together here. They appear exactly as they were recorded, retaining misspellings, syntax, unusual use of punctuation and underlinings, and personal idiosyncrasies to preserve the immediacy, spontaneity, and flavor of the original diaries. After reading a few entries, the reader will begin to pick up the rhythm of the language of each diarist and will be able to identify each one.

Misspellings and syntax often give a clue to the way the men spoke—the way they pronounced the words was often the way they spelled them—and so you may detect local dialects as you read the entries. (For example, Horner never uses an "s" when referring to "several mile.")

Day by day, as Ware and Horner approach and fight at Gettysburg, the reader peers into the thoughts and experiences of two enemies until they are almost face-to-face. After two years of war and thirty-five days of intense marching along a hundred miles of hot summer roads, Thomas Ware and Franklin Horner end up fighting in the same battle south of Gettysburg. One is on the side of a hill later known as Big Round Top, and the other is just a musket shot's distance away, near a pile of boulders called by the locals the Devil's Den. This is as close to a vision across the firing lines as anyone has gotten who was not there.

It is interesting to remember that these two young men are personally involved in one of the most momentous and cataclysmic events in the history of the United States. As well, they were writing about what may have been the most important events to occur in their own lives. In fact, for one of these young men, the experience becomes as momentous and cataclysmic as his own death.

It is just as interesting to remember that these men are not professional soldiers. To them, participation in the army has been a one or two years' respite from their civilian identities—peacetime farmer and carpenter. They joined the army because it seemed like the thing to do or because it seemed a quick way to a promised steady paycheck for a while. Their diaries simply begin in 1861, with no reflections upon motives or expectations. Certainly the thought of death floated vaguely in their minds, but not with the grim resolution of the professional soldier. In a couple of years, the plan was, they'd be back to farming or woodworking.

From the entries it becomes obvious, almost from the beginning, that these two individuals are remarkably similar. Even though the sociosections of the United States in the 1840s, 1850s, and 1860s were, because of the primitive communications network, less able to interchange cultures than today, it appears from these two chronicles that young men at war ponder the same things: the weather; the discomforts; the food; the countryside they're seeing for the first time, or perhaps marching through again; the scenery; the pretty girls in towns they pass through; friends both old and new; and, of course, home.

In their diaries Horner and Ware mention many of the same things—especially the weather and the countryside—on the same day. They were often only a few miles apart, and a thunderstorm that soaked Thomas Ware's gray frock coat in the late morning was likely to dampen Franklin Horner's indigo sack coat early that afternoon.

They rarely mention high ideals, or patriotism, or glory, or causes, and never refer to states' rights, or the concept of the Union, or slavery—perhaps the politicians who stayed at home were "fighting" for those principles, but not these men. Eventually, the ultimate question must arise: Just why were they fighting—these strikingly similar young men—against each other, to the death?

The story of Gettysburg—the campaign and battle and resultant effects upon the nation's past and present—has been told over and over by trained historians, professional military men, and armchair tacticians. But these young men lived it—day by weary, often boring, occasionally terrifying day—and recorded what were to them the important details—receiving mail, writing

Saw Port the Irwin Artillery, I
with Several went to a house near
Camps & got a great many Cherries I
never Saw the like before, We are encamped
at the foot of the mt. Several gone over
it to look for horses, People mostly
poor & very thickly Settled, very good camps.
Capt Croft ordered to report at
Atlanta Ga as ass't Commissary, Sent a
letter by him to have mailed to Pa, wrote
a letter to "J.B.H.", singly out evening,
have a Splendid place to Sleep some dry
Straw, Had a Splendid nights rest,

July. 1st Wednesday.   1863,
        A cloudy day, We have
orders to prepare 3 days rations and
be ready to march at a moments
warning, Orders came to be ready
to leave a 4 Oclock, Soon the drum
beat and all in lines, Our
Brigade (Benning) in front,
We passed through the village of
Fayetteville Pa, we Bk

letters, having something to eat, pressing the hand of a friend, or surviving combat. The most important things, when it finally came down to the battle, were victory and survival—and often not in that order.

And, while the macrocosm of the Gettysburg Campaign has been laid down in well-chosen words with scholarly conclusions from decades of objective study, this is the subjective microcosm of the campaign and the battle, told on the spot—"from the hip" so to speak. It is the story of what happened within the hearts and minds of two youthful combatants caught up in one of the most famous and important battles in all of history.

If it is true that we only hear the winners' version of history, it is also true that we often read only the intellectual's version of it. Not so here. This is the soldier's version of one of the greatest battles ever fought.

Thomas Lewis Ware was born September 9, 1838, in Lincoln County, Georgia, to Nicholas and Matilda Stovall Ware.[4] Thomas was the firstborn of eleven sons and two daughters. For most of his life he lived and worked on his family's farm near Lincolnton, Georgia. In what was probably a wave of patriotic fervor for his newly formed country—the Confederate States of America— twenty-two-year-old Thomas Ware enlisted on July 14, 1861. Along with dozens of his friends from the county, Ware joined the "Lamar Confederates," named after Capt. Lafayette Lamar, who died before the first year of war was gone. Ware was enlisted "for the war unless sooner discharged." When the Lamar Confederates were mustered into what was to become the Army of Northern Virginia, they became Co. G, 15th Georgia Regiment of Infantry. Shortly after his enlistment, Ware began keeping a journal.

Ware was promoted from private to second sergeant on December 6, 1862, then to first sergeant sometime in March or April 1863. He was fairly literate, was acutely observant, and had a mind for details, but it wasn't necessarily for these qualities that he was promoted. In a system that was democratic but not always

---

[4] Thomas Ware's prewar biography comes from Mary W. Probst of Lincolnton, Georgia, a descendant of the Ware family still living in Thomas's hometown.

militarily effective, Confederate officers up to a certain rank and noncoms were elected to their positions; thus it was probably his popularity with his fellow soldiers that won him the promotions. His journal entries on the dates he was elected show pride at gaining the higher ranks.[5]

In December 1862 his younger brother Robert Andrews Ware transferred from Co. B, 6th Alabama Infantry, to Co. G, 15th Georgia, presumably to be with Thomas. To celebrate, they had a "feast" of potatoes.[6]

Ware and the men of Co. G, 15th Georgia, participated in several major battles, including Garnett's Farm and Malvern Hill during the Seven Days Battles, Sharpsburg (called Antietam in the North), Second Manassas, and Fredericksburg. Ware's service records show that he was present for duty from the day of his enlistment, never having been either sick or wounded during his association with the Confederate Army. His diary entries prior to those included herein, however, have Thomas complaining of various ailments, including jaundice for two weeks in December 1862 and a high fever on January 23, 1863, which caused him to be on the sick list for the first time and to be given two doses of quinine for the first time in eight years. Chronic toothaches bothered him from May 1862 until he finally had six teeth "plugged" and three extracted in Richmond in February 1863. Dr. Blankman did the work and charged Ware $40.[7]

Franklin Horner was born September 22, 1836 (or 1837— records differ), in Cameron County, Pennsylvania, the son of Jonas and Mary Horner. He had at least one younger sister, Louisa, born six years after him. His military papers show that he was a carpenter by occupation and that he was five feet, eight inches tall, with a fair complexion, blue eyes, and light hair.

He enlisted on July 21, 1861, in Co. H, 12th Regiment Pennsyl-

---

[5] Ware Diary, December 6, 1862; March 2, 1863.

[6] Ibid., December 9, 1862.

[7] Ibid., December 10, 1861; May 20, 1862; February 2, 1863. The Thomas Lewis Ware Diary is fascinating in itself and contains many heretofore unknown facts about common soldier life. Reference will be made again to it later, as it is the purest form of primary source documentation.

SATURDAY, JUNE 27, 1863.

took up the line of march at six Oclock this morning crossed the Potomac at edwards ferry then went as far as the mouth of the monocacy where we encamped about four Oclock for the night marched about fifteen mile rained a little nearly all day the boys in good spirits nothing from the front

SUNDAY 28

Took up the line of march at six Oclock and crossed the monocacy and marched through buckestown and bivouac the little army corls where we encamped about one Oclock the weather was clear and all day we marched about fifteen mile through a fine wheat country the wheat is ready to harvest

MONDAY 29

had orders to march at daylight but did not start till one Oclock we went in rear of the wagon trains all day went past frederick city we got to camp about 11 Oclock we marched about ten mile through a thriving wheat country had a little rain nothing from the front we are now nearly a day behind time so we lost we made it up in marching bags of time vania Reserve Volunteer Infantry. At the very moment Horner was signing the papers, unbeknownst to him, cannons were roaring and men were dying as the Battle of Manassas (or Bull Run, as they would call it in the North) was being fought that day in Virginia.

Probably because he was one of the older men in the outfit—in his mid-twenties—Horner was promoted from corporal to first sergeant on August 3, 1861. The regiment was mustered into service at Harrisburg, Pennsylvania, on August 10 of that year.

On June 27, 1862, Horner was captured at Cold Harbor, Virginia, in a battle called Gaines Mill. After five weeks as a prisoner in Belle Isle Prison in Richmond,[8] he was exchanged (a system used early in the war of trading prisoners so they would not jam up the prisons) and rejoined his regiment on August 6, 1862.

Franklin Horner's military records show that he was wounded at the Battle of Antietam, September 17, 1862. It was apparently a slight wound, since he never even mentions it in his diary. By the summer of 1863, he was well enough to be working with his regiment on the fortifications outside Washington.

He was still working on those forts and rifle pits and writing faithfully in his diary in June 1863, when Confederate general Robert E. Lee and his Army of Northern Virginia, fresh from a string of victories including Fredericksburg in December and Chancellorsville in May, slipped away from Gen. Joseph Hooker's Union Army of the Potomac and began a move northward on an invasion route.

A collision course was now being set.

---

[8] The June 27, 1862, entry in Thomas Ware's diary states that he hears fighting at "Coal harbor," the battle in which Horner is captured. Later, Ware sees the group of prisoners captured at Cold Harbor. Perhaps his eyes rested for a moment on Franklin Horner.

Horner's route, June 1

Monday, June 1

Morning butiful, got orders to march at 7 O A. M. to morrow, after dinner orders came for us to march at 7 P. M. at
7 O clock we were in line marched through the city the boys
cheering the whole way; we got to upton's Hill Va, about
twelve O clock P. M. where we stayed till morning

Franklin Horner

June the 1st. "Monday." 1863.

Cool & pleasant day. Received orders to leave at 6 A. M. &
go back the same way we came & near the same old
Camps. "<u>Bennings</u>'s" 2nd in front. We marched quick time.
We marched the same road rested only 3 times going
within 2 mile of our former Camp. We stopped near a large
pond in a piece of woods, water not plentiful, at 1 P. M.
marching only 10 miles. Brigade guard placed around; &
now all the boys resting themselves finely; Received a letter
from "<u>C. W. P.</u>"

Quite a warm & pleasant night. We drew 3 days rations,
bacon flour & peas

Thomas Ware

T he war, after two years and almost two months, has taken a
heavier toll on some Union units than on others. Franklin
Horner and the men of the 12th Pennsylvania Reserves,
since February, have been ordered to the defenses being built
around Washington, the capital of the North.[9] Though his unit's

---

[9] Bates, Vol. I, 885. "In February, 1863, the division [to which Horner's regiment
was attached], now reduced to a mere skeleton, was ordered to the defences of
Washington."

orders for this day were to prepare for marching by tomorrow, the men are ordered to march this very evening—not the last time orders will be changed at the last minute for Horner and his regiment.

He doesn't detail their exact route out of Washington, but from where they halted at midnight—Upton's Hill on the Virginia side of the Potomac—we can assume they crossed the Long Bridge out of Washington, a very common route for Union armies heading into Virginia.

The Long Bridge spanned the Potomac at approximately the same place U.S. Route 1 crosses it today over the George Mason/Rochambeau Memorial Bridge. Washington has undergone a great deal of change since the Civil War, and many of the areas that were once water have been filled in and contain parks and public grounds. A very active imagination would be needed to picture the Potomac the way Franklin Horner's regiment saw it in June 1863.

Thomas Ware and the men of the 15th Georgia are about twelve miles southeast of Culpeper, Virginia, some sixty miles to the west of Franklin Horner and his unit. The "Benning's 2nd" he refers to is the brigade of Georgians commanded by Brig. Gen. Henry "Rock" Benning, the brigade to which Ware's regiment belongs.

Both Union and Confederate armies used generally the same method of organization. An army was divided first into several corps, each of which contained three or four divisions, which contained four or five brigades, which, in turn, contained four or five regiments. Each regiment comprised ten companies, which, on paper at least, contained one hundred men each. Attrition had, by the time of the Gettysburg Campaign, reduced company strength to about forty men.[10]

Ware's concern for the lack of water is a real one. Soldiers became incredibly thirsty on the march, especially in the summer, even when carrying canteens. Anyone who has hiked long distances, such as ten or twelve miles in one day, knows that the thirst

---

[10] Ware's July 30, 1862, entry records that "we have 44 fit for duty." His November 8, 1862, entry states that his company has forty-two men in it. Obviously, some freshly recruited units would have been larger, nearing the prescribed one hundred per company. Practical thinking (supported by statistical evidence) tells one that from the moment the unit leaves the mustering-in station, a few men will be ill or missing. Beware of anyone who says they know exact numbers.

continues into the night. The men in the ranks also needed water in camp to cook their food and wash.

The three days' rations Ware drew that night were typical in a Civil War army on the march. The men would nearly always cook everything up at once so it would be available for immediate consumption on the march. Often they would eat as much of it as they could at that first meal, reasoning that the provisions carry lighter in your stomach than they do slung across your shoulder in your haversack. As they marched through friendly country south of the Mason-Dixon line, the Confederate soldiers could rely on sympathetic farmers and townsfolk to hand out what food they could spare to hungry troops.[11] Once they entered enemy territory, the story was a little different.

Pork or bacon was a staple in both armies, as was salted beef, dried vegetables, and soft bread or flour. But provisions, like everything else in the military—both Union and Confederate—were subject to the same bureaucratic foul-ups that have beset armies since more than two or three soldiers first banded together to make war.

Of the numerous first-person accounts of army life in the American Civil War, one of the classics, both enjoyable and enlightening, at least from the point of view of the Union soldier, is John D. Billings's *Hardtack and Coffee: The Unwritten Story of Army Life*. (It is significant that he named his book after foodstuffs, apparently the first thing that came to mind after twenty-two years out of the army!) Billings divides rations, in quantity and type, into "camp" rations and "marching" rations.

Camp rations—at least for the Union soldiers—were superabundant, including twelve ounces of bacon or pork or one pound, four ounces of fresh or salt beef; and one pound, six ounces of soft bread or flour or one pound of hard bread (known in both armies as "hardtack"), or one pound, four ounces of cornmeal. In every company of one hundred men there would be distributed a large quantity of peas or beans, rice or hominy, green or roasted coffee or tea, sugar, salt, vinegar, pepper, potatoes, and

---

[11] Ware Diary. Numerous previous entries in Ware's diary mention "the boys" going to nearby homes to buy meals and other provender from locals.

molasses. Vegetables and fruits often came dried and compressed: "desiccated" in the official nomenclature of the army quarter-masters; "desecrated" to the common soldiers.

Marching rations, on the other hand, consisted of three-quarters of a pound of salted pork or one and one-quarter pounds of fresh meat, a pound of hardtack, coffee, sugar, and salt.[12]

The Confederate counterpart of Billings's book is Carlton Mc-Carthy's *Detailed Minutiae of Soldier Life*. On the subject of food in the Confederate Army, McCarthy's most certain statement is the uncertainty of the food situation. Often they would have an abundance of bread and no meat or plenty of meat but no meal or flour. Sugar would appear in great quantities, but there would be a dearth of coffee. While Billings states that in the Union Army it was the exception and not the rule for a soldier to go longer than thirty-six hours without food, McCarthy says that for a soldier in the Confederate service, one day without food was common, two days were not uncommon, and sometimes three and four days were endured without army-issued food.[13] Confederate rations were similar to but simpler than those given to the Union soldier. Confederate accounts speak frequently of biscuits, pork, and beef, and "slosh," or "coosh," made by mixing flour and water with boiling bacon grease. It is no wonder that "foraging"—begging or, more often, stealing—was more common in the Confederate Army than in the well-supplied Federal Army.[14]

And it is understandable why hungry Confederates would be eager to attack a Union camp. McCarthy, as well as other Confederates in numerous battles in which they overran Northern camps, lists among the spoils of war barrels of coffee, bread cooking in the oven, roast beef, canned peaches, lobsters, oysters, tomatoes, milk, liquors, Havana cigars, and fine wines.

---

[12] Billings, 111–13.

[13] The Ware Diary entries for May 3, 1863, reveal him complaining of nothing to eat in thirty-six hours, having marched sixty miles with only one meal. By 8 A.M. May 4, they had marched forty miles "since yesterday am with nothing to eat." The first food they got was a box from home with sausages, butter, potatoes, ham, and light bread after fasting two days. That day they drew two days' rations: ". . . of course, the 'Co' eat it all at one meal."

[14] I include McCarthy's and Billings's accounts as typical of army rations so that the reader may compare them with Ware's and Horner's comments on food.

Finally, Ware mentions receiving a letter from "<u>C. W. P.</u>" He has worked out some elaborate code for someone special from back home. In earlier entries he mentions receiving letters from "<u>A. B. C.</u>," then "<u>D. E. F.</u>," then "<u>G. H. I.</u>," and so on. It was not uncommon for correspondents in the Victorian era to hide the identity of loved ones. From his continued coded references, one can assume that Ware had a special young lady waiting back in Lincolnton for his return.[15]

---

[15] Ware Diary, September 21, 1861; October 6, 1861; October 30, 1861; December 5, 1861; December 19, 1861; January 18, 1862; February 1, 1862; February 22, 1862. Ware's coded references to the letters continue intermittently throughout his diary at regular intervals. There was obviously someone with whom he was involved at home.

Tuesday 2

This morning the boys look like old soldiers again our camp ground was celected this morning where a regiment had been encamped. the day is warm and pleasant the boys are nearly all away too get somthing too eat, evening cloudy look like rain nothing new to day

Franklin Horner

June 2nd. "Tuesday." 1863.

Pleasant day. "Co" drill & Batt. in Eve. Our Camps are in a very rough thicket. Wrote a letter to "C. K. R." No news from Vicksburg only that "Grant" was falling back & Joe "Johnson" preparing to attack him, nothing confirmed. "Vallandigham" reported to be in our lines.

Raining at dark, all preparing Shanties, needing rain very much.

Thomas Ware

It was not unusual during the Civil War for different units to use the same area for a campsite. In fact, it was not unusual for enemies to occupy the same campsite within hours of one another. The most famous such incident was on the 1862 Maryland Campaign, when first Confederate, then Union troops occupied the same campsite; a Union officer discovered Lee's campaign plan wrapped around three cigars at a campsite that had been previously used by the Rebels.

Campsites usually had a few bare essentials: plenty of water for horses and men; dry, fairly level ground; and wood for fires. Often when a campsite is mentioned in a diary or an account, one can determine approximately where the soldiers camped by looking for large flat areas with a stream nearby.

Franklin Horner mentions that many of the boys are away

getting something to eat. They've had to resort to foraging, raiding some local wild blackberry patches, or imposing upon local farmers for what is needed. As both armies begin to move and time to cook rations is short, there will be more foraging.

Thomas Ware has spent part of the day drilling, a tedious necessity of being a soldier. Tactical maneuvers were practiced over and over until they could be performed under the most rigorous conditions, such as on rugged terrain or during the chaos and deafening confusion of battle.

Civil War tactics as taught at West Point and propagated through the army to volunteer commanders in "Tactics Manuals" were precise maneuvers that began on the level of the individual soldier and evolved up through companies, regiments, brigades, and divisions. The manuals were superfluously worded, leaving nothing to the imagination as to how a command should be interpreted by the individual soldier; and if all battles had been fought under ideal conditions and every soldier perfectly trained, the Civil War battlefield would have looked as if someone had orchestrated a grand dance, with blocks of men wheeling and turning in precise order.

But battles are not dances. They are roaring maelstroms of confusion and horror. Orders are issued, transmitted, and obeyed by men who are a breath away from eternity in an atmosphere of near panic, where hardly anything can be heard and nothing interpreted calmly. Additionally, while the command is on its way from one level to the next, couriers are slain. Death kills the message when it kills the messenger before the command reaches every segment of the battleline. But those are, in nineteenth-century parlance, the fortunes of war—things that cannot be helped. One thing the officers could control, even to a small extent, was how their men would understand and execute orders. Drilling the men helps, and more drilling helps a little more, so this isn't the last time you will hear of Ware—or Horner—at drill.[16]

---

[16] Ware Diary entries. August 6, 1861: "Drill. . . ." August 9, 1861: "Drilling as ever." August 12, 1861: "Drill. . . ." August 14, 19, 21, 26, 27, 28, 1861: "Drill. . . ., Drill, Drill. . . ." August 29, 1861: "Drilling as ever." Drilling continued on a more intermittent basis through 1862 and 1863. Franklin Horner, though he doesn't mention it as often, doubtless drilled just as frequently.

Ware also mentions Grant at Vicksburg. The war is going on in other theaters around the country. Ulysses S. Grant and his army have surrounded the important town of Vicksburg, Mississippi, the last major bastion of Confederate resistance on the Mississippi River. Should Vicksburg fall to Union troops, the North would control the entire Mississippi River and will have cut the Confederacy in two. The siege is so important that even Thomas Ware, a typical common soldier in another Confederate army as far away as Virginia, is aware of the action in Mississippi and its consequences.

Clement L. Vallandigham was the leader of the Peace Democrats in the North, otherwise known as "Copperheads." They were an active political party in the North with pro-Southern sympathies. Vallandigham had been arrested and convicted in May of expressing treasonable sympathies toward the South, then banished to the Confederacy. But even the Confederacy didn't want him; Jefferson Davis put him under guard as an "alien Enemy." Later he was shipped to Canada.[17]

Ware mentions the men preparing "shanties" because it was raining. Sometimes also known as "shebangs," these were makeshift lean-tos made out of whatever cover the men could put together—two shelter tent halves, their gum blankets, wood, tin from a nearby shed, even branches and leaves from trees—anything to keep the rain off. And yet, though rain meant more work when preparing to sleep, Ware knew all too well, as did soldiers of both armies, of the misery of marching when the weather is extremely dry.[18]

When Ware talks about needing rain, it's not for the crops. Dust rising from a marching column gets in eyes, noses, and mouths and sifts down collars, shirtsleeves, and trouser waists to end up acting like sandpaper wherever moving arms or marching legs touch clothes or skin.

---

[17] Long, 349, 358, 361, 364.

[18] Numerous photographs are available showing extensive and quite creative use of indigenous foliage by the soldiers. Thomas Ware mentions in his July 5, 1862, entry that because of the heat, the men built "brush arbors."

Wednesday, June 3, 1863

raining some this morning the boys look rather hard they look almost as hard as they would if they had been marching for two month, the weather is clear this afternoon and warm no tents yet, expect some to morrow, all well

Franklin Horner

June 3rd. "Wednesday." 1863.

Cloudy, But little rain fell during the night. No drill today as 'tis damp. Requisition made out for clothing for the "Co". An address at Major "Bird's" by Col. Harris of 2nd Ga & Capt "Parks" of 17th. Ga on Christian Association. A. Gullatt & J. Remson arrived in Camps from N. C. where we left them sick. "Gullatt" not exactly well of the Small Pox. All very glad to see them as we had no idea we would see them so soon.

W. B. Sims died in N. C. with Small Pox, all regretted his death very much as he was loved by all, he had no enemies. Abb. & Jim escaped through the enemies lines & crossed the "Chowan" river. Jerry "Crawford" joined the "Co" is quite an unhealthy man, & will get a discharge.

Received orders to prepare 3 days rations & be ready to leave by day tomorrow. All buisy cooking most the night.

Thomas Ware

It is no wonder "the boys look rather hard" to Franklin Horner. Rain was one of the greatest discomforts a soldier living without shelter tents could endure—surpassed, paradoxically, only by the lack of it. While dry weather made marching and moving uncomfortable, rain made encamping miserable. Clothing was wet, shoes and blankets soaked, food sopping, and wood for heat and cooking practically unburnable. Arms and ammunition were wet and needed to be cleaned and dried as soon as possible, drinking water was muddied, and the very ground upon which a soldier had to sleep was a quagmire. Horner was no doubt relieved when the weather cleared in the afternoon.

Thomas Ware had a more frightening problem: smallpox in camp. Of the approximately 620,000 Americans who died in the Civil War, two-thirds were casualties of disease rather than enemy bullets. When small-town boys like Horner or rural farmers like Ware were jammed together in the army for the first time in their lives, without immune systems built up from exposure, communicable diseases ran rampant. During the Civil War, diarrhea could waste a young soldier's health for weeks on end until dehydration and death finally took him.[19]

Ware mentions requisitioning clothing for the company, one of his duties as first sergeant. At the beginning of the war, most companies in the South were provided with uniforms from their hometown areas: either their original militia uniforms, which they had worn for a number of years prior to the outbreak of war, or special, newly made uniforms to wear for the next several months until, as many mistakenly believed, the war would be over and the men would be home. With each hometown providing uniforms, it is no wonder that at the beginning of the war there was nothing "uniform" about them.

Later, gray became the official color of the Confederate uniform, but procuring gray cloth and manufacturing uniforms on a massive scale was something the fledgling Confederate States' government simply could not accomplish. As their original uniforms wore out, common Confederate soldiers such as Thomas Ware were often sent clothes from home, dyed a butternut brown in a sincere attempt to turn the clothes gray.[20] Existing photos of

---

[19] There were crude attempts made by the army doctors at preventive medicine. On November 18, 1862, Ware records that "I with several others were vaccinated today from T. 'Albea's' arm." This indicates that the doctors had a rudimentary knowledge of communicable disease and the buildup of antibodies. On January 17, 1863, however, Ware complains he was vaccinated for the fourth time and none had taken.

Georgia troops show a variety of uniforms in cut and color, from the short, waist-length shell jacket, to a longer sack coat, to the thigh-length frock coat. And as the war progressed, and even though the men of each company attempted to maintain uniformity, the uniforms became a mottled collection of grays and browns, with differing hats and trim. And although Ware has made out a requisition for clothing, it is difficult to tell when—or if—the men will ever see the uniforms.

Ware mentions an address made by some officers belonging to the Christian Association, one of the many religious organizations that circulated through the camps, both North and South. The United States during the 1850s and 1860s was a passionate place, as the speeches and broadsides that still exist prove. A wave of religious fervor swept the country during the decade preceding the war, and men were converted to, schooled, and baptized in Christianity, then went out to slay their brethren with a vehemence worthy of an Old Testament "army with banners." Thomas J. Jackson, whom we know now as "Stonewall," would lead his men in praying for the souls of the enemy, then lead them in battle to send those very same souls on to eternity as if they were lambs for the Sabbath sacrifice. Several general officers were ordained ministers. It was an odd balance of perceived duties to God and country, but they could live with it.[21]

According to the muster rolls listed in Lillian Henderson's *Roster of Confederate Soldiers of Georgia, 1861–1865*, Vol. 2, Absalom J. Gullatt, after his escape across the Chowan River in North Carolina, would eventually die of pneumonia in Richmond in 1864 and be buried in Hollywood Cemetery there. (Three other Gullatts,

---

[20] In his November 12, 1862, entry, Ware mentions receiving some boxes of clothing from Richmond. On November 13, 1862, he receives "a pr pants shirt &c from home" and says, "All living finely; not so much from the government." And on November 17 he buys a pair of pants from the army quartermaster. Apparently, as with the food, it was a case of "feast or famine," since in his October 30 entry, he mentions that some of the boys are barefoot.

[21] Ware mentions camp meetings often throughout his diary. Perhaps his May 25, 1863, entry reveals his attitude about them: "Another good meeting, but marred by a political speech of 15 minutes which made it worse." While Ware may be fighting for Christian ideals as expounded upon in "meetings," he obviously dislikes the interjection by anyone of politics into his life in the army.

including a cousin, also served in Co. G, 15th Georgia Infantry. The Wares and the Gullatts apparently became close during and after the war. The last son born to the Ware family in 1864 was named Peter Gullatt Ware.[22]) William B. Sims is listed as having died in White Mills, North Carolina, but Jerry Crawford survived the war to surrender with the army at Appomattox. James Remson had two brothers, both officers in the company, and he survived the war to surrender at Appomattox.[23]

Once again, rations have been issued—probably late in the day—and Ware writes, apparently late at night, as they cook the rations in preparation for marching.

---

[22] Mary W. Probst, correspondence with the author, December 1989. Mrs. Probst is the grandniece of Thomas Ware.

[23] Henderson, 454–60.

Thursday 4

cool this morning. Clear and warm all day, the war news are not very encourageing to day, except that Gen Stoneman made another successful raid clear around the rebell army and destroyed a great amount of property, got no tents to day. we have a pleasant place for our camp. health good in camp all quiet.

Franklin Horner

June 4th. "Thursday." 1863.

Fine morning. Drums beat before day for all to be up & ready to march by light. We got but little sleep (as we were up cooking 'till 11 P. M. & then aroused at 3 A. M.) Quite a stir around early, called in lines & left at sunrise in the direction of "Raccoon" ford. (A. Gullatt unwell and left with a pass at a private house)

After a march over a rough road mostly plantation road, we came to the ford, most of us waded it, some crossed on the dam. (At this place we crossed last Aug.) We marched slowly going the Culpeper C. H. road. Water very scarce & very hot & dusty. We rested often. After a march over a hilly road we stopped to Camp at 1 P. M. near the C. H. in the same or near the same Camps we remained in (March) '62.[24] We marched 12 miles. Brigade guard placed around.

Gen'l "Longstreet" passed through Camps, the boys cheered him. All resting themselves finely, pleasant & warm night. Abb. came to Camps, did not succeed in getting in a Priv house as the family was afraid, had a good nights rest.

Thomas Ware

Ware's route, June 4

". . . we came to the ford, most of us waded it, some crossed on the dam."

Franklin Horner may be referring to Union Cavalry general George Stoneman's raid between Richmond and Fredericksburg, the only major cavalry raid Stoneman undertook, prior to his writing, that actually took place during the Chancellorsville Campaign, May 1–4, 1863. In fact, by the time Horner writes this entry, Stoneman had been replaced by Gen. Alfred Pleasanton, who reorganized the entire Union Cavalry Corps of the Army of the Potomac into a much more effective fighting force. The effects of Pleasanton's reorganization will soon be experienced by Thomas Ware and the men of the 15th Georgia.

―――――

[24] In the March 12, 1862, entry, Ware refers to his campsite near Culpeper as being "in a very thick pine thicket" about one mile from town.

Even though Ware was up cooking until 11:00 P.M., he and his unit had to be ready to march at sunrise, which meant arising at 3:00 A.M. One thing a modern student of the Civil War must keep in mind is that daylight savings time was not in effect during the summertime in the nineteenth century as it is today. Modern times for sunrise and sunset must be adjusted by one hour in order to get the proper perception of lighting on the battlefield and march.

For example, Gen. Richard Ewell's attack on Culp's Hill at Gettysburg in the evening of July 2, 1863, did not get under way until about 7:00 P.M. their time. As Johnson's Division made its way across Rock Creek and began moving up Culp's Hill, it became so dark by 8:00 P.M. that they had to halt, fearing the enemy could be hiding in ambush in the darkness.[25] Had daylight saving time been in effect that July, he would have had another hour of daylight; however, in 1863, by 8:00 P.M. it was as dark as it is today by 9:00 P.M. ("Stonewall" Jackson used darkness to his advantage at Brawner's Farm on August 28, 1862, when, badly outnumbered and anticipating reinforcements, he waited until 6:30 P.M. to attack.[26] He knew that if he got in trouble, he would only have to hold off the enemy for an hour and a half before darkness at about 8:00 P.M. would necessitate a cease-fire.)

This also means, of course, that sunrise came an hour earlier, so when Ware writes of marching at sunrise, he probably means about 4:30 A.M. his time, or 5:30 A.M. daylight saving time. It is also important to remember that individual watches were set to different times and kept different times. When reading first-person accounts, the best indications of time are mentions of daylight, sunrise, or dusk. On a Civil War battlefield, darkness is all that matters in terms of time; it is a rare instance when battles were fought into the darkness.

Raccoon Ford is on the Rapidan River, and from Ware's remarkable powers of observation, we can reconstruct his movements and the approximate location of his campground from the beginning of June until his march to Culpeper.

---

[25] Coddington, 428. Long considered the premier book on the campaign, *The Gettysburg Campaign: A Study in Command* is a superb reference work.

[26] Gaff, 66.

Examination of nineteenth-century military maps in the *Atlas to Accompany the Official Records of the War of the Rebellion* (Pl. LXXXVII, 2) does not reveal the location of the dam, but the maps do indicate a mill listed under the name of a "Col. Porter" just downstream from the ford. An on-site inspection of the area of Raccoon Ford turned up the remnant of a dam, and the Rapidan in this vicinity has an "island" of logs, mud, and trees that has grown up over the years. According to *Historic Culpeper*, a 1974 work published by the Culpeper Historical Society, a large grist and flour mill was located just below a dam on the Rapidan but was washed away in a 1937 flood.[27]

Fords across rivers were very important to travel in nine-teenth-century America. A ford was merely a shallow section of a river, usually bottomed with rocks, where wagons carrying pro-duce to market could cross. Wagon and horseback traffic would naturally carve a road to the ford, and settlements would arise where there was commerce passing. The village of Rackoon (as it was first spelled) Ford was just such a place. In fact, in 1738 the first Orange County Court House was built at the ford on the south side of the Rapidan River.[28]

Although the ford traffic has since been rerouted to a bridge built nearby, traces of these roads can sometimes still be seen. Dur-ing wartime, when bodies of troops or supplies had to be rushed from one side of a river to the other, fords were guarded carefully, and many minor skirmishes and an occasional battle were fought over the possession of a vital river ford.

After the death of Gen. Thomas J. Jackson, through the month of May 1863, Gen. Robert E. Lee reorganized his Army of North-ern Virginia into three corps to be commanded by Generals A. P. Hill, Richard S. Ewell, and James Longstreet. Longstreet com-manded the First Corps, to which Thomas Ware's unit belonged.[29] Longstreet was a popular commander, and it was always a thrill for a private soldier in the ranks to get a glimpse of these famous men who were orchestrating their movements. Cheering a popu-lar officer like Longstreet or Lee was common.

[27] *Historic Culpeper,* 133.
[28] Ibid.
[29] Coddington, 12.

Longstreet had just been in consultation with Lee concerning the movements of the army. Ware didn't realize it, but when Longstreet rode past, he was carrying a secret that would change both Ware's and Horner's lives forever: The Confederate Army of Northern Virginia was about to invade the North for the second time in less than a year.

"After a march over a hilly road we stopped to Camp . . . near the C. H."

Friday 5

Morning clear and pleasant, we were told that the tents would be here to day, but they did not come, and we have too ly in the dust the best we can and still we have to come out on dress parade like as if we came out of a band box, my health is not good,

Franklin Horner

June the 5th. "Friday." 1863.

Apperance of rain. Received orders for all to be ready to leave by 8 A. M. to see the "Cavalry Review" 3 miles beyond "Culpeper" C. H. We were in lines & awaited for marching order. "<u>Roberson's</u>" <u>Brig</u> of Cavalry passed by us. We soon left, passing through the village with music, down "<u>Coleman</u>" St. as far as the Hotel, thence filed right up Spencer St. The town is a very desolate looking place, a great many houses in ruins, but few citizens could be seen. We marched along the R. R. for 3 miles when we came to the Review ground on the R. R. near "<u>Brandy Station</u>", the field was large the day was very dusty & warm. Each Brig stacked guns along the R. R. a guard stationed beyond & none permitted to go beyond, so the track for several miles was crowded with soldiers & hills, the cars came down full, tops crowded with girls. There was over 2000 citizens, a great many girls several on horseback. Several the girls rode up & down the road accompanied with officers at full speed (as the road run parallel with the R. R.) The girls could ride faster than the men. The girls are great riders in this country. There was near <u>12,000</u> Cavalry present on the field. Gen'ls "<u>Steuart</u>" & "<u>Hood</u>" rode up & down the lines & reviewed the troops. The scene was a rich one & worth seeing they made several splendid charges. The Artillery

Ware's route, June 5

fired 160 <u>Shots</u>. Evry thing passed off finely, we suffered very much with heat as the day was warm & no water near. The review lasted 5 hours & all left for Camps, the road very dusty. Cloudy & apperance of rain, we marched back the same road & arrived in the same Camps at 6 P. M. all very much pleased. Sprinkling rain a little, very much needed. Cloudy night but no rain. "<u>Lazenby</u>" remained late with us in Camps.

Received a letter from home, they have fine crops of wheat. No sick, & all resting finely. Good nights rest.

Thomas Ware

Franklin Horner's frustration with the military was growing as his health deteriorated. Even in the summer, sleeping out in the cool air and early morning dews have an effect upon a soldier's health. His terse entry reveals anger at a military that expects them to be clean and neat, with weapons dry and in order, after spending four nights sleeping on the damp ground.

The previous afternoon, Thomas Ware had gone into camp just outside the town of Culpeper, the county seat of Culpeper County, Virginia. Culpeper County was formed from Orange County (the county south of the Rapidan River) in 1748, ten years after the Orange County Courthouse was built at "Rackoon" Ford. Some five million acres were originally the Virginia estate of Lord Fairfax, who had employed young George Washington to survey his vast holdings. This estate was eventually confiscated by the colonists when the Revolutionary War began. The county was active in the Revolution, condemning the British Parliament and forming a military unit known as the Culpeper Minute Men. This Revolutionary War organization was resurrected in 1860 (for the coming "revolution," no doubt) and became Co. B, 13th Virginia Infantry. Two other companies were formed from the men of the county: the Little Fork Rangers, who were cavalrymen, and the Brandy Rifles.[30]

During four years of civil war, the county was crisscrossed by

[30] *Historic Culpeper,* 1.

both armies, and two major battles and several skirmishes were fought there. The Battle of Cedar Mountain took place in August 1862, and Ware refers to it later. As well, Confederate general A. P. Hill was born and grew up in Culpeper, and John Pelham, the handsome Southern artillerist from Alabama, died here after the Battle of Kelly's Ford in March 1863.

The town of Culpeper did not begin to be called that until 1870, but since there was a county courthouse located in the town, which was then called Fairfax, it was more often referred to as Culpeper Court House.[31]

From old maps and with the help of local historians, we know that Coleman Street was sometimes called (and is now renamed) Main Street. The Old Virginia Hotel, which existed from 1846 until 1907, stood on Coleman Street. Ware and the men of the 15th Georgia passed the hotel, then turned right on Spencer Street, which leads out of town and directly to the railroad tracks of the Orange and Alexandria Rail Road, now called the Southern Railway.[32]

The men marched along the railway until they reached a large, open field. In the classic work *Lee's Lieutenants*, Vol. 3, in a footnote on page 1, Douglas Southall Freeman includes a reference to a book by Maj. Daniel A. Grimsley, *Battles in Culpeper County Virginia*. On page 8, Grimsley states that the review held on June 5, 1863, took place on the Auburn Estate. He refers to a furrow being made as a demarcation line about three hundred yards west of the railroad, extending in a line parallel with the railroad: ". . . along by the broad spreading elm tree that stood in the flat in rear of the grave yard, on the Ross estate, quite to the run . . . The horse artillery . . . was formed in batteries along the ridge in rear of, and on the west side of the branch . . . General Lee occupied a little hillock, immediately on the west side of the railroad, some 300 or 400 yards North of the station at Inlet."[33]

During the Civil War, the Auburn Estate was owned by John Minor Botts, who is said to have won the place in a poker game.[34]

---

[31] *Historic Culpeper*, 4–5.
[32] Interviews with Rosemarie Martin of the Culpeper Historical Society and J. Russell Guinn, 1990.
[33] Freeman, 1.
[34] *Historic Culpeper*, 37.

Botts, although a Virginian, was a Union sympathizer, and so photos taken by Northern cameramen showing Union officers quartered there are abundant. The name Botts appears on the *Atlas to Accompany the Official Records of the War of the Rebellion* map (Pl. XLIV, 3), so we know where the review took place and where Lee stood to watch. The review ground was north of the tracks, and since Ware says that they stacked guns along the tracks and a guard was placed beyond, we can surmise that Ware and his comrades stood along the south side of the railroad tracks to watch.

The famed Confederate Cavalry leader "Jeb" Stuart (whose name Ware misspells) had planned a review of his cavalry corps for his commander, Gen. Robert E. Lee, most likely to assure the commanding general that his cavalry was prepared for the upcoming summer campaigns. Unfortunately, Lee had to cancel his appearance for the review at the last minute. The indomitable Stuart invited nearby army units and held the review anyway. Ware got the opportunity to see not only Stuart, but also Gen. John B. Hood, his divisional commander.

There was always a rivalry between the footsoldiers and the mounted cavalrymen. "Hey cavalry, come out o' them boots—I can see your ears wiggling!" or "Come out from under that hat—I know you're in there, I can see your legs a-danglin'" were some of the jibes footsore infantry tossed at passing cavalry. No doubt Ware jeered at a few of the cavalrymen who passed in review and received all the attention from the pretty girls of Culpeper County.

While it may have been a good show, it was for nothing. Lee later sent word that he could attend a review on June 8, and the cavalry brightened metal and soaped saddles all over again. For some reason, Ware and the men of the 15th Georgia were not invited to the second review.[35]

From Ware's route out of Culpeper, we can determine approximately where the campsite of the 15th Georgia was located. If he marched down Coleman Street, passed the hotel, and turned right, we can surmise his campsite was south of the hotel that was on Cameron Street and Coleman. According to the 1835

---

[35] This is surprising, since most accounts list Hood's Division as being present for the second review.

Thompson Map of Culpeper,[36] much of the area west and south-west of West Street was undeveloped. Mountain Run meanders through the relatively flat area (which today remains undeveloped). Later, Ware mentions crossing the railroad to get to Pony Mountain, so we know he was west of the railroad as well. A famous photograph of Union camps in Culpeper was taken from the present site of the National Cemetery, which is east of the railroad. Obviously, Ware's unit did not use this old Union campsite. Most likely, they were in the area west of Culpeper and used the Mountain Run flatlands for their camp, not only this time but in March 1862 as well.

---

[36] *Historic Culpeper,* insert.

Saturday, June 6, 1863

cool this morning our tents came at last, our camp begins to look like a camp again, nothing new to day my health is some better to day have no dress parade this evening the boys are all busy fixing their tents for sunday, all quiet in front

Franklin Horner

June the 6th. "Saturday." 1863.

Pleasant day. Received orders to wash & clean our guns & be ready for Inspection tomorrow. 9 A. M.

Received orders to cook 3 days rations & be ready to leave at 12 A. M. So we have 3 days rations of flour to cook & no cooking utensils. All very buisy, very warm day. Rumors are that we will cross the river tonight. Evry thing in motion. All in lines at 12 A. M. line formed in the road. We stacked guns & awaited 1 hour for the <u>Div</u> to form. We marched through the town the same way & route we did yesterday with music. Stopped near the review ground to rest. Here it rained a small shower which greatly refreshed evry thing, as the roads were very dusty. We then left & marched opposite the review ground & filed right through a large piece of woods (a country road) leading in the direction of "<u>Stevensburg</u>". Came in the main road at a Mill near the village leaving it to the right, going through the fields thus cutting off 2 miles. We then marched quick time the same road we marched the 21st of <u>Aug</u>, <u>viz</u>; the "Madison" C. H. & "<u>Kelly's</u>" ford road, which road we marched 5 miles, it now dark, we then filed right & took the "<u>Ellis</u>" ford road & marched 3 miles & stopped to Camp at 11 P. M. it as dark as "<u>Erebus</u>" evry one so tired Just fell out & lie down with orders to leave in 2 hours. (As we were to cross

the ford & attack the Enemy) the order was countermanded
by 2 A. M. that the Enemy had fallen back at "Fred'burg"; &
thus our long & wearied march was in vane. All quite wet
& no fires allowed, of course we suffered & some got but
little sleep. But verry little by myself. 15 miles today.

Thomas Ware

When Franklin Horner says that his camp is beginning to
look like a camp again, he means that the tents are all
lined up in rows, in what the soldiers called company
"streets," which could be traveled from one part of the camp to
another.

While Horner may not be as prolific in his writing as Thomas
Ware, a careful reading of his entries will nearly always provide
some insight into his mood, be it frustration, excitement, or apprehension. In his mood we can probably read, in general, a reflection
of the mood of his fellow soldiers.

For cooking and winter housing purposes, a company was
broken down into several smaller, informal units, each called a
mess. A mess usually consisted of four messmates who would
somehow divide up the responsibilities of building winter quarters or procuring and cooking food and cleaning up afterward. In
January 1862 the other boys in Ware's mess were Privates Anderson Glaze, Thomas D. Hawes, and John B. Callaway. By March 24,
1862, Glaze and Callaway were no longer with Ware's mess, but
were replaced by Absalom J. Gullatt and William B. Sims.[37]

The messmate system had been around since the Roman legions conquered most of the world, and its purpose has not necessarily been merely cooking. The preparation and consumption of
food fills some spare hours and breaks up the soldiers' day. More-
over, it provides an excuse to sit face-to-face with other human be-
ings and, in the midst of what is, for the most part, rampant inci-
vility, reminds the soldiers of home and family. It gives the men
something to look forward to, and it bolsters the group identity.[38]

---

[37] Ware Diary, January 17 and March 24, 1862, entries.
[38] Holmes, 128.

You're likely to fight harder to help a man with whom you've broken bread.

For soldiers, there seems to have been—and continues to be—a phenomenon that can only be described as a "brotherhood of suffering." Poor food, lousy living conditions, sore feet and muscles, heavy burdens to carry unending miles on the march, sickness, wounds, and death all contribute to a feeling of family between warriors. One combat veteran put it this way: "I realized that Company K had become my home. No matter how bad a situation was in the company, it was still home to me. . . . I belonged in it and nowhere else." Perhaps not so surprisingly, this was written in 1981 by E. B. Sledge, a marine veteran of World War II.[39] In the Civil War, and especially in Confederate units, this was even more the case, since the men were recruited from the same geographical area. Often, within Southern units, some men were literally family.[40]

Ware and his messmates had no cooking utensils because, in anticipation of their movement, they had loaded all their heavy equipment onto the company wagon. The wagons took off, taking with them the utensils.

It is hard to imagine the apprehension that Ware and his comrades-in-arms must have felt, force-marched through the night, expecting a battle at any time, and finally discovering that the enemy has withdrawn. Officers worry, first about getting their men primed for battle, then about keeping them on edge for too long.

Ware's writing switches from present to past tense and back again through this and other entries. You can almost see him pulling his treasured journal out of his haversack as the column halts for a few seconds and scribbling quickly, "it now dark," without even enough time to make his thoughts grammatically correct. Reading Ware's and Horner's diaries is like being in that dark column of tired soldiers or sitting by the fire outside the tent, listening to their thoughts as they idly compose them into prose for posterity.

---

[39] Sledge, 101.

[40] Henderson, 454–60. There were at least twenty-five families with two or more brothers or cousins of the same last name represented in Ware's Co. G, 15th Georgia, over the four years of war.

Ware's route, June 7

Sunday 7

cooll for this time in the year can not account for it, have Regimental inspection at eight O clock, the colonel is not pleased that the guns are not in good order, the boys had no place to keep them in the dry since we came here till now. no war news to day health good have church at falls church Chap Miller preached for us

Franklin Horner

June 7th. "Sunday." 1863.

Clear & pleasant morning, all up by sunrise & formed a line in the road, & about faced (which showed plainly we were going back)

We marched back the same road we came yesterday, marching slowly, only we marched through "Stevensburg", marched through "Culpeper" C. H. up "East" St. with music. 15th Ga in front the Brig. "Rhoads" Div was marching down "Coleman" St the same time. Arrived in Camps (same old Camps) at 12 A. M. & rested, all very tired. "McLaw's" Div encamped near the town & was in our front, "Early's" Div. also near the town. John Arnett came to our "Co" to see us, his Reg'mt near.

We drew 3 days rations & all very buisy cooking. Several Companies up nearly all night. Quite a cold night, slept but little.

Thomas Ware

While the fact that it was a Sunday never entered into whether an army would march, fight and kill, or rest, for Horner this particular Sunday was one of rest and reflection. He was obviously caught up in his frustration at the military: The army had first held up delivery of tents, causing the men discomfort and illness, then reprimanded the soldiers for weapons that were not in good condition because of exposure to the elements.

Ware as well was slave to the whims of officers and military exigencies. Anxiety over the march toward the enemy and the unknown possibilities of combat was replaced with frustration as the men were turned around and marched back to Culpeper, victims of faulty military intelligence or a realistic feint by the enemy.

While it seems that Horner and Ware were wrapped up in "soldiering," it must be remembered that there were some motives for their having made this commitment in the first place. Perhaps when they originally signed up they had believed, like most of the country, that it would be a short, relatively bloodless war. The fact that they both signed up within two months of Fort Sumter meant that they had probably been beguiled by a recruiting officer and the newspaper reports that a major battle was shaping up somewhere in Virginia west of Washington. Ware may have been influenced by the fact that his younger brother Robert in Alabama had enlisted on May 7, 1861.[41] A careful reading of both diaries reveals no reason for enlistment given by either. Perhaps what is most remarkable is that nowhere in either diary, in two years of daily entries, does Ware write about slavery or states' rights or Horner about reunion or rebellion.

They both have ample opportunity. In fact, the issue that they were supposed to have gone to war over—slavery—is never mentioned as such. And when the two write about their direct experiences with blacks, their reflections are surprising.

Two days after his enlistment in July 1861, Horner takes a "jaunt" through Harrisburg, the capital of Pennsylvania, and makes the statement, "I will pretend to describe it as there are more negros in the place then would make a good picture for every other person you see is a negro." Again, on July 28, 1861, as they pass through Baltimore, he records the large number of "negros" as compared with whites in the city. On April 27, 1862, in camp

---

[41] Georgia Department of Archives and History, Service Records of Civil War Soldiers.

near Catlett's Station, Virginia, he writes that there are "Plenty of contrabands coming in." (Union general Benjamin Butler began using the Southerners' view of slaves as property against them, declaring that any escaped slaves who found their way into Northern lines would be considered "contraband of war" and therefore subject to confiscation by the federal government. Escaped slaves during wartime soon gained the nickname "contrabands" from the Northern soldiers.) Horner describes them as carrying all their worldly possessions on their heads in bundles and says that they are exceedingly happy, ". . . thinking they are going to the land of plenty."

But the next day he complains because the contrabands are using the railroad cars to get to Alexandria, Virginia, but the soldiers who wish to use the cars need a pass.[42]

And at least once during his stay near Cedar Run south of Culpeper, Virginia, Horner realized that not all blacks were welcoming their liberators: ". . .went to a house that was on a hill with a beautiful grove in front everything had a fine appearance I stoped and enquired if I could get dinner and a negro wench said I could not get anything to eat there so I turned and left came to the conclusion that the proprietor was a seccessionist."

This is not to say that Horner was prejudiced, or at least any more prejudiced than his Northern contemporaries. If anything, he displayed the same racism shown by the majority of white Americans from the Northern states who grew up seeing few blacks in their society.

Thomas Ware, in his diary entry on July 1, 1862, after the Battle of Malvern Hill, writes that, "I talked with a few of the wounded of the 7th Mich. who told me this was called by them a political abolitionist war." Granted, the men of the 7th Michigan were disgruntled at being wounded and captured, and by no means can their individual statements be taken as an accurate survey of the feelings of a majority of Northern soldiers. But the fact that they would complain about it to the enemy, and that Ware seems to be saying, in using the plural, that the Michigan men he talked to were not alone in calling it a "political abolitionist" war, would

---

[42] Horner Diary entries on dates cited.

indicate that a number of the men of the 7th Michigan felt that way.

Ware's feelings for the blacks he sees are, if anything, neutral. Whether his family owned any slaves is unknown. Ware writes, on March 26, 1862, that he received from home a box of sausages, three hams, "pinders," and cakes, all sent by "negro 'Steve.'" He doesn't elaborate, but certainly doesn't imply that Steve was owned by the Ware family. On February 15, 1862, he notes that, "Our mess hired a free boy today, for 15$ pr. month."

Ware was impressed enough at one situation he witnessed to record it on June 29, 1862, after the fight at Garnett's Farm: "One case I must mention, a negro was seen with a gun bringing a Yankee to Gen'l Toombs." In other words, a black captured and turned over to the Confederate Army one of the soldiers who was to be freeing his race.

Ware was grateful for the help of a black man who helped him and Absalom Gullatt find their way out of the Dismal Swamp, where they had gotten lost during the Suffolk Campaign on April 16, 1863: "We wandered about in the swamp & woods some time, at last saw a dim light some distance ahead. We went to it and found a free negro there, who piloted us out to the main road." Six days later, on April 22, 1863, in describing the hardships of the population around Oak Grove Church in northeastern North Carolina, he writes, "people once very wealthy but now all the negroes gone to the enemy. . . . These wealthy people have been roughly treated by the Yankees, who after taking the negroes & property from them were placed under guard & kept there by a negro sentinel." One gets the impression that "negroes" were for the wealthy, a class that the Wares, with eleven children by 1863, may not have been a part of.[43]

Regardless of whether Ware's family owned slaves, it is obvious from his diary entries that Ware is at least one Confederate soldier whose reasons for fighting did not include slavery.[44]

---

[43] Ware Diary.

[44] I have included in this section all references to blacks to be found in both diaries up to July 1863. That's it: a total of five references each to blacks, and no references to the great evil that precipitated the war—slavery. While slavery may have been a major cause of the war, only 7 percent of all Southerners owned slaves, and it certainly wasn't the reason that either of these two common soldiers were fighting.

According to American Heritage's *The Civil War* (31), of the six million whites in the South in 1850, only 5 percent, or 347,525, owned slaves; only .6 percent (37,662) owned twenty or more. The Wares were probably not in either category.

Monday 8

very cool this morning for this time in the year we have good news from the army. Hooker is crossing the river again. all quiet in camp boy in good spirits we fixed our tent to day, health good the news from grants army is not very encourageing for the last few days.

Franklin Horner

June 8th. "Monday." 1863.

Fine morning. "Earley's" Div passed by Camps at 8 A. M. Saw John Frazer George Gullatt & several others in the 60th Ga. Troops passing most the day. "Ewell's" Corps passed by & through the town comprising "Roads" "Earley's" & "Trimble's" Div. Expecting orders constant to leave. Finished cooking rations by 3 P. M. Received orders we would remain all day & clean up &c. Winfrey "Arnett", an old friend remained with me this Eve & all night, was very glad to see him. All quiet & no talk of leaving. I was with Billy Elliott's "Co" tonight. J. Watkins came to Camps been absent 5 months, not yet able for duty. Very cool night.

Thomas Ware

"Hooker" is Maj. Gen. Joseph Hooker, the commander of the North's Army of the Potomac, one of the several Union armies and the one closest to Washington. Horner, ensconced in the environs of Washington, was interested in the activities of the Army of the Potomac—Hooker's army—because he had marched and fought with them. In fact, General Hooker was his Corps Commander at the Battle of Antietam.

Hooker had made a foray across the Rappahannock River to find the Confederates. The movement had little effect upon Horner's regiment since it had not yet been assigned to be a part of the main army, but it was this very demonstration that Horner describes that put Thomas Ware's unit in motion on June 6.

Horner is also concerned with the news from Grant in Mississippi. Who knows where camp rumor starts, but as close as Horner's unit is to Washington, the more likely the rumor is to be true. In reality, Grant's siege in Mississippi was going well, with the Union grip around Vicksburg inexorable, the Confederates unable to break through the siege lines, and many of the inhabitants of Vicksburg living in caves to avoid the Union bombardments.

The 15th Georgia was stationary on this day, and Ware had the good fortune to be visited by several of his friends.

Recruiting during the Civil War was done on a parochial level; often classmates or members of a local militia unit or fire company would all sign up together and, when mustered in, would stay together as a unit for the duration of the war. The Confederate Army tended to keep the men from the same state together all the way up to the brigade level. In other words, Ware's Co. G, which was recruited in Lincoln County, Georgia, was put in the same regiment—the 15th Georgia Volunteer Infantry—as Co. H, recruited from Hart County. Other companies were pulled together from nearby counties in that geographical section of Georgia, until the 15th Georgia had its full complement of ten companies. Then the 15th Georgia was put in a brigade with four other Georgia regiments. Some believed the men fought better when grouped together by state.

The practice of placing regiments from the same state in brigades together occurred in the Union Army as well, but seems not to have been quite as widespread. Toward the end of the war, the Union Army would ship regiments where they were most needed to refill decimated brigades and would fill regiments with both volunteers and draftees. Confederates clung to the parochial recruiting system until the end, and it was sadly evident that local counties were being bled dry of their youth as veteran regiments shrunk pitifully. Eyewitnesses to the surrender at Appomattox recalled seeing the Confederate column crowned with regimental flags, which were seemingly more numerous than the men.[45]

---

[45] See pages 195–98 for an analysis of the effects of the war on families in Lincoln County, Georgia.

The system Ware fought under, of placing hometown friends together, had its good points and its bad. In camp, from the very first day, there was always someone around that you knew. In battle, you knew that if you were wounded, a friend would be there to take care of you, and if you were killed, to make sure you got a decent burial in a spot someone would remember—morbid thoughts, perhaps, but ones that have crossed many a soldier's mind.

Maj. Gen. Joshua Chamberlain, in his *Passing of the Armies*, lists common friendship as one of the reasons for courage: "... as a rule, men stand up [for one another in battle] from one motive or another—simple manhood, force of discipline, pride, love, or bond of comradeship—'Here is Bill; I will go or stay where he does.'"[46]

You see it in modern wars as well. William Manchester, in *Goodbye, Darkness*, his moving memoir of World War II in the Pacific, explains why he left the safety of a hospital to return to the front and his fellow marines—men whom he had known for only the time of his enlistment, yet with whom he was willing to die: "It was an act of love. Those men on the line were my family, my home. They were closer to me than I can say, closer than any friends had been or ever would be. . . . Men, I now knew, do not fight for flag or country, for the Marine Corps or glory or any other abstraction. They fight for one another."[47] It seems a verity that echoes through the centuries of human conflict.

But on the bad side, when lifelong friends or blood relatives went into battle together, marching shoulder-to-shoulder, and one goes down with a wound or is killed, it is all the more horrifying to the survivor.

In previous entries, Ware refers to men from the company returning after being ill or captured. This had a very important unifying effect—much like the men dining together or the "brotherhood of suffering" mentioned before—and helped boost the men's morale. Though Ware doesn't discuss it in detail, he frequently writes of friends visiting or returning to the unit. E. B. Sledge, although writing about a different war, makes a point that nonetheless is universal: "Men who recovered from wounds and returned to duty nearly always came home to their old company.

[46] Chamberlain, 20.
[47] Manchester, 391.

This was not misplaced sentimentality but a strong contributor to high morale. A man felt that he belonged to his unit and had a niche among buddies whom he knew and with whom he shared a mutual respect welded in combat. This sense of family was particularly important in the infantry, where survival and combat efficiency often hinged on how well men could depend on one another."[48]

Ware had an additional concern: Since December 1862, his younger brother Robert Andrews Ware had been in his company. Robert had been a schoolteacher, apparently in Alabama, before the war.[49] He had originally signed up with the 6th Alabama Infantry in Montgomery on May 15, 1861. Thomas Ware's diary records several visits by his brother.[50] Robert applied for a transfer to Co. G, 15th Georgia, on September 2, 1862, but the papers didn't come through until December 7. In the uncertainty that is inherent in war, the two brothers could now look after each other on the march and in battle.

There were times, sitting around the campfire at night, when the boys talked of home and what they would do when they returned. It is easy to imagine Thomas Ware, after finishing supper, sitting with Winfrey Arnett, or the Gullatt brothers, or the Cawleys or Remsens, and talking about life in Lincolnton before the war came. Then the conversation turns to what they will do once they get home: pick up the plow once more . . . or never again; start a dry-goods store with the army money they've sent home; marry and have children . . . a whole schoolhouse full of children. . . .[51]

But in war, a mere ounce of soft lead or ten pounds of whistling ordnance can shatter dreams forever.

---

[48] Sledge, 101.

[49] Robert Ware Diary. Not the writer Thomas was, Robert kept a diary for only a very short time. Ken Norman, a relative by marriage to Thomas and Robert Ware and a descendant of the Normans mentioned in Thomas Ware's diary, has read it and documents the fact that Robert taught school briefly before joining the Confederate Army.

[50] Ware Diary, January 13, 14, 15, and November 9, 1862, entries.

[51] Ibid., October 7, 1861: "Night has come, we sit up quite late & had a fire before our tent. We sit & talked about the several incidents & our 'loved ones.'"

Tuesday, June 9, 1863

nothing more from Grants army to day. Hooker still has one Division on the other side of the river watching the rebels, the magezine of Fort lyons blew this afternoon— and killed and wounded nearly all that were in the fort at the time, weather is pleasant but windy all day health good all quite in camp

Franklin Horner

June 9th. "Tuesday." 1863.

Pleasant day, W. Arnett left for his Camps early. Heavy Cannonading this morning below "Brandy Station" & about "Kelly's" ford. Enemy succeeded in crossing at 2 places & drove our Cavalry-back some distance. Cannonading lasted most the day. While we were drilling we received orders to leave immediately. We formed a line & stacked guns & awaited for orders to leave, which soon came. We marched near the town & marched back near the same way, crossing the R. R. & marched back towards "Raccoon" ford 2 miles & then filed left across a field & came in the "Stevensburg" road near the mountain & formed a line in an open field exposed to the hot sun, at 12. A. M. formed a line of battle. Part the Div marched to our rear & formed a line at the foot of the Mt. We put up blankets as shelters & thus protected us from the burning sun, here we remained 'till dark & was then ordered back to our former Camps. The fight was very desperate all Cavalry on both sides, casualties not yet know a great many prisoners taken on both sides.

Thomas Ware

Fort Lyon was a link in the chain of forts built around Washington to help defend it. It was located southwest of Alexandria, about seven miles from where Horner was located. The explosion of the magazine in Fort Lyon was a tragedy, but it was overshadowed by the events in Culpeper County, Virginia, where Ware was stationed.

The Battle of Brandy Station would become known as the largest cavalry battle ever fought on the North American continent. It is a bit surprising how quickly the details of the battle get to Ware. Obviously, Ware is writing on the evening of June 9. He's correct that the enemy managed to get across the Rappahannock River at two places: Beverly Ford and Kelly's Ford. He's also correct in stating that the Union Cavalry drove the Confederates back a good distance. In fact, they had caught the renowned Confederate Cavalry commander Jeb Stuart with his guard down, relaxing a bit after the two big reviews he had just had. Stuart refused to believe even some of his own commanders when they told him, during the battle, of the extent of the Union Cavalry's incursion.

The interruption of drill and subsequent rapid marching of Ware's unit stems from the action at Brandy. At some point during the battle there, Stuart or some other officer had apparently decided that they'd better get infantry ready to come to their support. According to Ware's description of their march, he and his unit ended up near what is named Pony Mountain on contemporary maps. The battle ended, however, before they were needed, so Ware and his unit returned to their camps.

After fighting nearly all day—a good deal of it hand-to-hand—and with more than fourteen hundred casualties on both sides, Stuart drove off the impudent Yankee cavalry and maintained possession of the field. In the Civil War, at the end of a fight, if you remained on the battlefield over which you'd fought, it was taken as a sign of victory. Stuart's on this day was a hollow victory, though. It was not the stunning victory he usually won over his Northern counterparts; something was changing in the mien and mettle of the Union Cavalry, which he would see again soon.

Wednesday 10

calm and pleasant this morning. no change in the war news Grant is still at Vicksburg and banks at port Hudson both places will soon be in our posession nothing from Hooker's army health good in camp all quiet along out picket line, our men are diging rifle pits all day

Franklin Horner

June 10th. "Wednesday." 1863.

Fine morning, all quiet in Camps, heard a few particulars of yesterdays fight. Our loss small, the Cavalry fought hand to hand & was desperate on both sides. We captured near 500 prisoners & horses. Gen'ls <u>Fitz</u> "Lee", & Col. "<u>Hampton</u>" reported very badly wounded. The intention of the Enemy was supposed to make a raid & find out where most our army was.

Some important moves are on hand both armies in motion & will soon meet. "Co" drill today all passed off finely in Camp nothing but Reg'mt <u>Inspection</u>.

Beawtiful eve. Geo. <u>Stovall</u> in Camps looking well &c. We drew 2 days rations & buisy cooking them as we have a standing order allways to have 2 days rations cooked. Apperance of rain tonight.

Thomas Ware

If Franklin Horner has heard about the Battle of Brandy Station, he doesn't mention it now or later. Instead, he talks about U. S. Grant at Vicksburg and Gen. Nathaniel Banks at Port Hudson, both fighting on the Mississippi River. Grant was tightening the siege around the small town hanging on the bluffs of the Mississippi, lobbing a virtually endless supply of shells into the town, continuing to make life miserable for not only the soldiers there, but the civilians as well.

Both Horner and Ware realized the importance of Vicksburg and Port Hudson. Should one fall, combined armies would concentrate on and force the other to capitulate. Then the Mississippi could flow "unvexed to the sea," and the Confederacy east of it would be forced to fight on two fronts, cut off from the Confederacy to the west. Supply and logistics would then be virtually insurmountable. Strategically, much was balanced upon the stocky shoulders of U. S. Grant, far away but close in the thoughts of even the private soldiers of both sides.

Horner's unit was digging rifle pits, a seemingly never-ending duty for the troops stationed around Washington. Eventually the entire Capital would be ringed by entrenchments, which, with but a small garrison, were supposed to hold against enemy attack upon the seat of government. It was hard work: digging and hauling; felling trees; and making log breastworks, bomb-proofs, huts, and parapets.

Again Horner mentions General Hooker's Army of the Potomac. If the Confederates continued northward, it would be Hooker's army that would have to challenge them to battle while somehow staying between them and Washington. Should Lee's army get around Hooker or defeat him in the field, these very entrenchments Horner was working on would be vital in protecting the Capital.

Horner's confident comment about both Vicksburg and Port Hudson soon being in the possession of Union armies is prophetic. Both would fall within a month.

Yet Ware's entry still has an undercurrent of hope. He recounts what he has heard about the cavalry battle at Brandy Station, and his account is remarkably accurate, although still reflecting the Confederate side of the story. H. B. McClellan, on Jeb Stuart's staff, said that Confederates captured 486 Union prisoners.[52] Ware is right when he says that Lt. Col. Frank Hampton—the brother of Gen. Wade Hampton—was badly wounded; he was later to die of his wounds. But the Lee who was

---

[52] Freeman, 13n.

wounded was not Gen. Fitzhugh Lee but his cousin, the son of the commanding general, William Henry Fitzhugh Lee, called "Rooney." It is easy to see how Ware might have become confused or perhaps was referring to Rooney but calling him by the name he rarely used.

Ware, too, seemed to be hearing, in an almost eerie way, the winds of premonition. He'd been a soldier long enough to have the soldier's prescience of what is likely to be.

One thing he couldn't see was the horrible attrition rate of Southern officers, often too brave for their own good. In both the cavalry and the infantry, brigadier generals often fought like common privates, leading their men into the thick of the fighting instead of ordering them to go. As they fought like their men, so they died. Privates could be replaced; highly trained, intelligent, educated leaders like Hampton and Lee could not.

Thursday 11

sent some of our boys to day a gain to work at the rifle pits nothing new from Grants army. Hook still has one Division on the south side of the river our Regiment goes on picket this evening at five O clock our company went to falls church is cloudy this evening but warm looks like rain health good

Franklin Horner

June 11th. "Thursday." 1863.

Cloudy morning, no rain fell during the [unfinished]

We were aroused before day by a little sprinkle, all up & made shelters but no rain fell. "Co" drill, no news all quiet in Camps. Nothing important from "Vicksburg" the Enemy still hold their same position. All await with anxious hearts the result. The fight at "Brandy Station" the 9 the hardest fighting ever done by Cavalry, loss heavy on both sides.

Asa <u>Lockhart</u> came to Camp from Hosptl, been absent 7 months. Rec'd a letter from Rev <u>Steed</u>, all quiet tonight.

Thomas Ware

While we can be sure that what Ware and Horner wrote about in their diaries were true personal experiences, we can also be sure that their days were filled with tiny, myriad details that never made it into their writings.

How many times during the course of a day did Horner talk with Sgt. Thomas W. Dick before Dick left on recruiting duty? How often did he report to Captain Bolar before Bolar's wounding at Fredericksburg or talk and joke with Henry Shuman or Oliver Sproul before they were killed in the fierce fighting for South

Mountain? Did Horner go off foraging or to church with Francis, Harvey, and David Overdorff before Francis was discharged and before Harvey and David were killed at Charles City Crossroads and Antietam?[53] How often did he think about them in his spare moments during the day and miss their companionship but fail to record those times in his daily entries because he just didn't have enough room?[54]

Since his brother's transfer to Co. G in December, Ware began to spend more time with him than he had since they were children.

Robert was born February 17, 1840, and so was about a year and a half younger than Thomas. The two were undoubtedly playmates as they grew up together in the woods and fields of northeastern Georgia in the 1840s. When the war first broke out, Robert was living and teaching in Alabama and joined the 6th Alabama Infantry. But since before September 1862, Robert had been attempting to transfer into the 15th Georgia. Thomas records numerous visits by his brother to the 15th Georgia's campsites, obviously to see Thomas but also to reacquaint himself with many of the boys he'd grown up with in Lincolnton.

One particularly pleasant stay occurred on January 13 and 14, 1862: "Brother Rob't & <u>Mr Mahone</u> came to see me, was very glad to see them as I hadn't seen him in 4 months. Snowed all night." The heavy snowfall forced Robert to stay all the next day and night. Robert visited at least two more times before finally joining Thomas permanently after receiving his transfer papers on December 7, 1862.[55] Both the 6th Alabama and the 15th Georgia were stationed near Fredericksburg, Virginia, at the time, so Robert probably had just a short walk down the lines to join his brother and boyhood chums.

---

[53] Bates, Vol. 1, 901–2. The war was particularly hard on the Overdorff family, which had two out of three boys that enlisted killed in battle within two and a half months.

[54] Horner Diary, September 17, 1862: "D. C. Overdorff was killed."; December 13, 1862: "Capt Bolar wounded." Though the references are brief, the fact that others in the company were killed during Horner's tenure in the service and he doesn't mention them indicates that he was probably closer to Bolar and Overdorff.

[55] Ware Diary, January 13, 14, 15, 1862; June 12, 1862; November 9, 1862.

Friday, June 12, 1863

seen nor heard any rebels last night came to camp this morning about five O clock no war news to day of any importance sergt Dick started on recruiting service to day, weather pleasant all quiet along our lines health good in camp Chaplain Miller went home yesterday

Franklin Horner

June 12th. "Friday." 1863.

Pleasant day "Co" drill.

Lieut <u>Stovall</u> in Camps; John Dunaway detailed as Division pioneer.

Nothing of interest transpired in Camps. We drew 2 days rations & have 3 days cooked & in our Haversacks, as we are expecting orders to leave constant. Beawtiful Eve & night. Very good nights rest. Apperance of rain.

Thomas Ware

John Dunaway must have proven himself handy with a pick and shovel or hammer and saws because he has been detailed to the Pioneers. "Pioneers" is the early-war term for engineer troops: the soldiers that actually carry out the orders of the engineer officers by building roads, fortifications, and bridges and performing other manual labor for the army. Yet being a Pioneer did not exempt one from danger. According to Henderson's roster, after having been wounded once at Fredericksburg, Dunaway would be wounded again at Gettysburg and at Chickamauga, Georgia, before being furloughed home. He was absent without leave on February 28, 1865, and disappears from the records.[56]

---

[56] Henderson, 456–57.

The last few entries should convince the reader that much of army life, even during an active war, was tedium. While Ware mentions it but Horner doesn't, they probably both had drill this day. They may have written some letters home, or gone foraging, or gotten into one of the many games of chance that were probably occurring around the camp. In camp on the march, rules apparently were more lenient, at least by 1863, and the men would often sneak off to fish[57] or get up a lively game of "ball"[58]—no doubt the forerunner to today's modern game of baseball, which has its roots in the American Civil War.

---

[57] Ware Diary, July 31, 1862: "boys off fishing and foraging."

[58] Ibid., February 9, 1863: "Boys buisy playing ball, all very lively." And again on February 12, 1863: "Boys amusing themselves by playing ball." One normally associates playing baseball with the Union Army, since Union general Abner Doubleday was credited with introducing the game to the army. In fact, Franklin Horner's diary entry of April 17, 1862, indicates the growing popularity of the new sport: "we have another game of ball this afternoon."

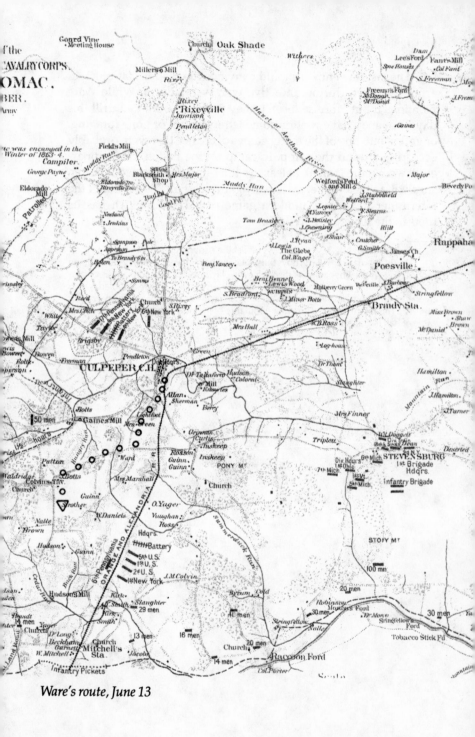

Ware's route, June 13

Saturday 13

Morning Cool and pleasant have no important news from the army to day, nothing doing in camp all quiet in front no rebels to be seen health continues good in camp have dress parade at 5 o rains a little this evening and cool

Franklin Horner

June 13th. "Saturday." 1863.

Fine morning. Orders are to wash & clean up & be ready to move & change Camps at 3 P. M. Several of the boys gone to the pond to wash.

Received orders to move immediately & be in lines in great haste at 11 A. M. not more than half the "Co" present. So hastily was the order we expected the enemy to be very near. Companies formed & marched near the Col's <u>qurts</u>, formed a line stacked guns & lie there 2 hours, soon all the "Co" came, & we soon found out that the Div. was going to change Camps. We soon in lines & left marched 3 miles South West of Culpeper C. H. the roads very dusty & very warm day, we suffered for water. We stopped to Camp near "<u>Cedar</u> Run" where the noted battle was fought, between "<u>Jackson</u> & <u>Pope</u>" & in a beautiful piece of woods near the latter's "head qurtrs" at 1 P. M. Rained a little during the Eve. I with several went out & got a great many <u>Cherrys</u>. We have very good water & Camps. Received a letter from Home, written the 6th.

Cloudy night with thunder & lightning.

Thomas Ware

Dress parade for Horner meant breaking out his long frock coat, polishing buttons, and cleaning muskets in order to be reviewed by his officers.

The Army Regulations of 1861 list the amount and types of uniform and clothing an enlisted man should receive over a five-year period. These include frock coats, four-button sack or fatigue coats, dress hats and forage caps, trousers, shirts, underwear, brogans or ankle high "bootees," socks, and an overcoat called a "greatcoat."[59] In fact, according to Horner's diary entry of July 26, 1861, after he is mustered in he drew his clothing: "one pr blue and one pr duck pants, two shirts, two pairs drawers, two pairs socks, one pair shoes, one blouse, one [unintelligible, but probably "tin"] cup, one great coat, one woolen blanket."[60]

Often, especially by 1863, the army would collect parts of uniforms that weren't appropriate for the weather and store them for the soldiers; if they didn't, the soldier would often "lose" the items somewhere along the march.[61]

Ware and "the boys," as he affectionately calls them, were preparing to move camp. An examination of Civil War period maps reveals no ponds in the area of Culpeper (which could merely be an oversight on the part of the cartographers) but does show a number of mills, which nearly always have a millpond nearby. The one closest to Ware's campsite is one owned by Mr. Gaines, about two miles southwest of Culpeper on Mountain Run.[62]

In his August 12, 1862, entry, Ware had mentioned hearing of Jackson's victory over Pope. The Battle of Cedar Run (called, variously, the Battle of Cedar Mountain, Slaughter Mountain, or Cedar Run Mountain) took place on August 9, 1862, when Maj. Gen. John Pope sent Nathaniel Banks's Corps of about eight thou-

---

[59] Todd, 41.

[60] Horner Diary, July 26, 1861, entry states concerning his swearing in, ". . . we swallow the grease or are mustered in the state service. . . ."—an interesting term for taking the solemn oath to become a soldier.

[61] Ibid., March 18, 1862, entry states that on a march to Catlett's Station via Bristoe Station, their route could be discerned by the number of overcoats discarded along the way.

[62] *Atlas to the Official Records of the War of the Rebellion (O. R.)*, Pl. LXXXVII.

sand men eight miles south of Culpeper to intercept "Stonewall" Jackson's force of about seventeen thousand men. Fighting swayed between the small stream of Cedar Run, where the Union troops were posted, and the mountain farmed by Mr. Slaughter, where the Confederates were stationed. General Pope did not arrive on the battlefield until Banks had been driven back to his original position north of Cedar Run. If Ware is not mistaken about camping near Pope's headquarters, then we know the men of the 15th Georgia set up their tents somewhere north of the stream.

Sunday 14

weather pleasant to day have company inspections at nine
O clock A M the boys go to church nothing new from the
seat of war to day have dress parade at five P. M. health
good in camp the boys in good spirits.

Franklin Horner

June 14th. "Sunday." 1863.

Cloudy morning, no rain fell last night. Have a guard
around the Brig & very strict orders. "Co" Inspection. A.
"Gullatt" quite sick. Preaching in Camps. We drew 2 days
rations & some cooking it. All quiet in Camps. Fine night,
all up late enjoying themselves.

Thomas Ware

A s they had the previous Sunday, some of Horner's fellow
soldiers went to Falls Church for services. Interestingly,
Ware had described in his diary entry of September 27,
1861 (which was before the Union Army had secured the Virginia
side of the Potomac River), his own unit's march to Falls Church,
the place Horner would visit numerous times a year and a half
later.

If Horner went to church with the rest of the "boys" this Sunday, he probably heard a good deal of preaching about the many
sins soldiers might succumb to, such as gambling, swearing,
lying, stealing, drunkenness, and being unfaithful to their duties
as soldiers, as well as the great sin of slavery. The men, no doubt,
all agreed with the minister about his list of sins and devoutly
promised to avoid all of them. Until Monday, at least.

The promise not to swear was probably the first to go, unless
the soldier had first gotten into a card game and then began

cursing at his bad luck. Getting drunk sometimes happened by accident. When the army occasionally issued whiskey as a ration, what could the preacher expect?[63]

Stealing from a fellow soldier could very well have been the worst thing a man could have done, with one exception: robbing the dead.[64] For the crime of stealing, men were made to carry a heavy log around camp for twelve hours or to stand on a barrel in the middle of camp for hours on end. Riding the wooden horse—a sharp fence rail suspended several feet off the ground—for a whole day with a sign around the soldier's neck proclaiming "Thief" would usually deter a second attempt at stealing. Perhaps one of the two worst punishments was being tied astraddle the wood-and-iron hub of the spare wheel on an artillery caisson as it rattled and bounded down the road on the march. The other feared punishment was being "bucked and gagged": having the legs drawn up with arms tied around them in a sitting position; a stick thrust under the knees and over the elbows, locking them into a cramped position; and a bayonet tied between clenched teeth. In a few hours men would cramp up excruciatingly, muscles screaming for release, occasionally descending into uncontrollable spasms and convulsions.

Cowardice under fire and chronic desertion often—though not always—brought capital punishment. In his March 5, 1863, entry, Horner mentions that two men were court-martialed for being absent without leave. More than a few times, Abraham Lincoln himself stepped in to commute some poor soldier's death sentence, much to the annoyance of the officers, who needed examples to deter further misbehavior.

---

[63] Horner Diary, July 28, 1861: "A few of the boys got a little too much of paddies eye water which caused them to be full of fun." Ware Diary entries, October 31, 1862: ". . . encamped at a brandy still at Mt hope. 3$ pr qt for brandy some boys got 'funy' finally a guard was placed at still." December 8, 1862: After some boxes from home came for Co. B containing brandy, ". . . the latter they partook of quite freely . . . All were up untill after midnight. Several of 'Co' 'B' & 'G' were seen 'hors d'combat' . . . the scene was quite amusing."

[64] Ibid., April 13, 1862: On this day he tours the battlefield of First Manassas with his captain. "A great many of our men were never buried but left lay where they fell . . . the bones of dead horses are thick all over the field. I have to acknowledge that some of our men are worse than barbarians. I seen them a grave open that rebel was buried in and tore the skeleton out and knock the teeth out for momentoes."

An execution by military firing squad was certainly an example never to be forgotten. Early in the war, according to the December 9, 1861, entry in Thomas Ware's diary, capital punishment was meted out to two members of the Louisiana "Tigers," a unit recruited by the courtly international soldier of fortune Roberdeau Chatham Wheat from the contingent of "wharf rats" who worked on the docks around New Orleans: "2 men of the 'Tigers' shot today for disobeying orders. Several of the Company went to see them shot." It left such an impression on Ware—whether or not he had actually witnessed the execution—that he mentions in his diary entry three days later that after going into Manassas for mail, he "came back where the 'Tigers' were shot."

Union officers, many of whom had attended the same military schools as Confederate officers, subscribed to the same brand of punishment for crimes. Thomas F. Galwey, an officer with the 8th Ohio Infantry, gave an account in his personal memoirs, *The Valiant Hours*, that is probably as typical as it is hideous.

The division to which his unit was attached formed a hollow square, open at one end, where two bounty jumpers from the 14th Connecticut were to be made an example of for the benefit of those entertaining the same notion. Two graves had been dug at the square's open end, which faced a hill. From the distance came the eerie refrains of the "Dead March." The division provost guard slowly approached, along with the provost marshal, the band, two chaplains, and two ambulances each carrying a coffin with the deserters riding upon them.

Halting at the graves, the deserters were forced to sit upon their own coffins before their soon-to-be sepulchers. Their sentence was read, their arms tied behind with light cord, and each was blindfolded. Galwey describes it thus:

> Then, after prayers by the chaplains, and all was ready, two firing parties from the provost guard took position in front of each victim. At a command from the Provost Marshall, the execution squads pulled their triggers. One of the two deserters was slightly wounded and fell over struggling on his coffin; the other was not hit at all but with desperate energy broke his pinion and snatched the handkerchief from his eyes.

A murmur of mingled pity and disgust ran through the division. Most of the pieces had only snapped caps. Here was either wanton carelessness in the Provost Guard or a Providential interposition to save the lives of the men. General French, the division commander, was in a rage at the awkwardness of the Provost Marshall and his men. The firing parties changed their pieces for others and fired again, the unhit man having again been pinioned and blindfolded; but with no other result, that we could see than again to wound the already wounded man, and to drive the other into a paroxysm of fear and trembling without even hitting him! An audible groan now passed through the division.

The left-hand squad fired once more, killing the wounded deserter, for he fell back upon his coffin and never stirred again. But the right-hand squad only wounded the unhit man at the next volley. He continued to struggle to free himself from his pinions.

The guns had evidently been loaded the evening before and had become wet from the rains which fell during the night. The Provost Marshall now brought up his men, one by one, and made them pull the trigger with the muzzle almost touching the unfortunate devil's head! But strange to relate, they only snapped caps, the victim shivering visibly each time. At last the Provost Marshal himself, drawing his revolver, placed the muzzle against the man's head and discharged all the barrels of it! This finished the man and he fell over into his coffin and never moved again. General French rode up. As we could plainly see, he was indignant at this clumsy butchery. Artists representing the New York newspapers or magazines made on-the-spot sketches of this horrid affair.[65]

---

[65] Galwey, 144–45.

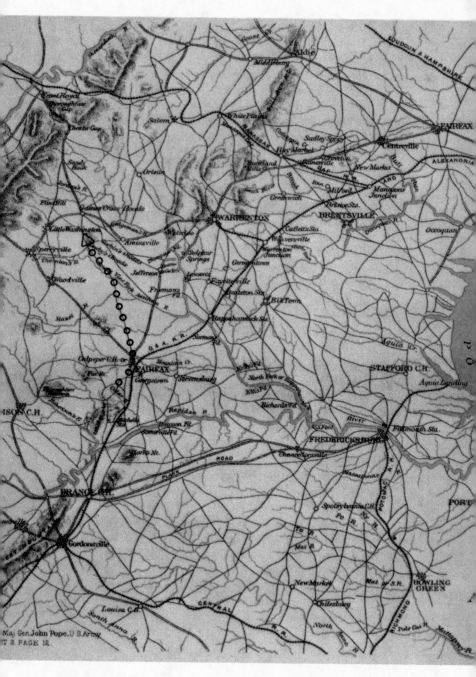

Ware's route, June 15

Monday, June 15, 1863

morning cool cloudy part of the day, rumors to day that the rebel army is going towards Maryland as fast as they can the President calls for one hundred thousand men for the defence of maryland & Penna nothing from Grants army. all quiet in camp health good

Franklin Horner

June 15th. "Monday." 1863.

Drums beat at day for all to get up & be ready to march at sun rise. All soon up & buisy preparing to leave. Several quite sick.

All in lines & left at the appointed time with 3 days rations. We marched back to "Culpeper" C. H. the same road we came Saturday. All the Division stopped ½ mile from the town, stacked guns & rested 1 hour & here we got orders to prepare for hard marching as we were going in the direction of "Winchester" on a force march.

We here drew 1 days rations of Crackers & now have 4 days rations. All those who was not able to march & sick would be left at the C. H. "E & W McCord" Murray Watkins & A. Gullatt" left, the latter very sick & looking badly. We passed through the town at 9 A. M. with music & marched 1½ mile beyond the town & took the "Front Royal" & Culpeper C. H. Turnpike. The waggons we left to our left going the "Winchester" pike the roads being better & we would leave the pike soon & go a very rough road. So the officers all carried their blankets with them as we would not be with them in several days, none but the Ambulance went with us. The pike as far as we marched it (which was 9 miles) was very good but very dusty, the day very warm water scarce. We suffered very much & I think was the hottest days march we ever taken, especially a force march. A great many fell out ranks overcome by heat & several sun stroke & some died, the road side was full.

We stopped & rested 2 hours in a shade at 2 P. M. the men broke ranks & fell about like hogs, so tired, hot & thirsty. We left at 4 P. M., hot & dusty, the country quite poor, few people living along the road, houses mostly deserted few farms in cultivation.

We left the pike at "<u>Hazel</u>" river, which stream we waded. From here on we marched a rough country road through a poor & rigid country large hills & Mts. This is "<u>Rappahannock</u>" Co. We stopped after crossing 1½ hour 'till 2 hours by sun & then marched over a very rocky road & waded "<u>Thornton</u>" river at dark. We marched 'till 9 P. M. very dark & a great many had fallen out. So we marched 18 miles the hottest days march I ever took. We lie down in an open field with orders to leave by light tomorrow, but little sleep by me.

Thomas Ware

For the first time, almost two weeks after it has begun, Franklin Horner mentions in his diary the Confederate invasion. Leading elements of the Confederate Army of Northern Virginia crossed the Potomac River this day and entered Maryland, and a contingency plan to raise an emergency volunteer militia force of one hundred thousand men from West Virginia, Ohio, Maryland, and Pennsylvania went into effect by order of President Lincoln. It would be another week—after the entire Confederate Army was streaming across the Potomac—before the reluctant volunteer warriors would feel the need to rise up under arms.

Suddenly, as the Confederate Army begins to move, Ware and the men of the 15th Georgia are drawn into the invasion. Their new campsite is abandoned and they return to Culpeper, passing through the town with their bands playing martial music. The wagons are sent a different route so as not to interfere with the troops' marching pace; officers are ordered to carry their own blankets and equipment for easy access rather than storing them in the wagons. The organized confusion of an entire army on the march begins to take over.

Today it would seem impossible for men simply walking along the road to suddenly pass out and die from sunstroke—something that certainly could be prevented. Yet, when canteens run dry and the day is hot and the men are burdened by equipment, death by overheating is not only possible but probable. And there was a certain purposefulness to this march as well: "Close up, men; close up." "No straggling." "Colonel, I want your men across the Thornton River by nightfall." Commanders at the head of a column following orders to push their men rarely see what Ware describes. During this day, Hood's Division will lose five hundred men falling out by the wayside, exhausted, overcome by one of the hottest days of the summer.[66] Ware sees just a small number of those who died.[67]

Who's to judge whether these poor men who died on the march from lack of water or too much sun were less patriotic than the men who were killed in battle or that their deaths were any more in vain than those of soldiers slain in combat? We have a tendency to think of soldiers' deaths as a gentle floating to the ground, wrapped in a sort of patriotic haze, brought on by a swift, clean bullet. But death in an army can stalk one disguised in myriad forms, from a childhood illness like measles, to a beesting, to the breathless convulsions brought on by too much heat.

Thanks to Ware's detailed observations of roads, towns, and streams, an analysis of most of his march route can be made. By comparing his observations, maps made during the war, and modern county maps, his odyssey from Culpeper along the invasion route can be followed today. Even more fascinating is the fact

---

[66] Tucker, 22.

[67] This wasn't the first or only time Ware saw men keel over from too much marching or drilling. In his diary entry for February 20, 1863, he states, "We march so fast that a report says several fell dead (I saw one)." Given the lack of proper nourishment, the overuse of tobacco, and the cursory medical examination upon recruitment during the Civil War, it is not so surprising that men would suddenly drop dead. Apparently, since it happened in February as well, hot weather isn't always needed to march a man to death.

that much of what Ware saw and describes along the way still exists. By following his route, either by automobile or on foot, the reader can literally travel in Ware's footsteps and see what he saw. It is a journey into time.

The wagons were probably sent along what is now modern Route 522, which leads to Front Royal, Virginia. Almost exactly a mile and a half north of the center of Culpeper, Route 729 bears off to the northwest, and almost exactly eighteen miles from Culpeper, it crosses the Thornton River in Rappahannock County, Virginia. Both correspond to roads on the map in the *Atlas to the Official Records* of the area.[68] The secondary road Ware took is indeed an undulating, hilly ribbon with granite outcroppings along its path, and it doesn't take much imagination to picture exhausted men falling out by the wayside, leaning up against the rocks in the shade, unable to take another step because of the mid-June heat.

---

[68] *Atlas to the O.R.,* Pl. LXXXVII, 2.

Tuesday 16

stiring news this morning from Pennsylvania, the rebels are going into the state as fast as they can Hooker is at Fairfax with his army likely this move of lees is the last or death strugle of the rebels, we went out and had a mess of cherries this afternoon weather warm health good

Franklin Horner

June 16th. "Tuesday." 1863.

Cool & pleasant day, not as warm as yesterday. I was too tired to sleep much last night, so but little sleep by me.

We were up at day & in a few moments in lines leaving at light, 15th Ga in front the Brigade. We marched over a very hilly & rough road for 3 miles & then rested 1 hour at which time Gen'l "Longstreet" & Staff passed us. The country along the road mostly poor, a few rich plantations & few farmes, most the citizen have left their houses & plantations. We soon came in the "Warrenton" & Front Royal pike at "Hains" X roads. We marched the Salem road for 2 miles & then filed left through the plantations, some places no road at all. We took a direct course, the waggons following the road.

Col "Rossier's" Cavalry passed us, various rumors in circulation some that "Ewell" had a fight near Winchester & whiped Milroy & had the latter about surrounded. Several prophesying as to where we are bound. We marched over hills & no road in few places, saw some fine fields of corn but little wheat along the road, & few people living along thro' this settlement. We marched 'till 1 P. M. & stopped on a high hill to rest, here we remained 2½ hours & then left going quite slowly for a few miles when we came to "Darby's X roads, from here to Camps the country was

Ware's route, June 16

quite rich but houses all deserted & fine plantations in ruins. All farms have rock fences, the road was very hilly & mountainous & very rocky & crooked roads. We marched down a valley between the Mt'ns, & now we are in "<u>Fauguier</u>" Co. A great many were sun stroke & I learn several died, the road side was crowded with wearied soldiers who had become overheated, the Evening was very warm & dusty. "<u>Rumbly G. Norman</u>" <u>Cover & D. Stevenson</u> of our "Co" all wearied & overcome by hard marching & very sick too were all left behind, about 100 of the Reg'mt left behind. We stopped to Camp at 9 P. M. at "<u>Marcum</u>" Station on the <u>Manassas</u> Gap R. R. 25 miles above the Junction where we encamped in an open field. Having marched 17 miles, we lie down with orders to be ready to leave by day break. Got but little sleep tonight.

Thomas Ware

Perhaps because he is a native Pennsylvanian, Horner reacts to the approach of the invading Confederates with alarm. Still, he is premature with his statement about the rebels in Pennsylvania. General Hooker, commander of the Army of the Potomac, has indeed moved his army in a direction that is indicative of how the Union Army will conduct the coming campaign: continually attempting to remain between the invading Confederates and the nation's capital at Washington. Robert E. Lee will try to pull the Union Army out of its position by threatening Pennsylvania cities, attempting to draw the enemy army into battle when and where he chooses—farther north, if possible.

It is remarkable that Horner feels that this invasion is the death struggle of the Confederate Army, especially after the several victories Lee had had just prior to this move. With the enemy invading his home state, could Horner have been whistling in the dark?

Ware's march takes him along another rough road, even more tiring this day because of his lack of sleep the previous night. He sees his corps commander, Gen. James Longstreet, again as the men rest.

He watches, perhaps with a little jealousy, the cavalrymen of Col. Thomas Rosser, who get to ride as they pass while he walks. He wouldn't have been jealous if he could have looked into the future: Rosser and his 5th Virginia Cavalry are headed for a battle the next day at Aldie on the Alexandria Pike.[69] The action becomes part of several days of severe cavalry fighting for Ashby's Gap. Ware hears the rumors—which turn out to be true—of a battle at Winchester, Virginia, on June 14 and 15 in which Union major general R. H. Milroy had his troops surrounded and captured by Confederate general Ewell's men.

The march takes the men generally along what is now Route 729 until they strike Route 522—the Warrenton and Front Royal Road—at Gaines (Ware calls it "Hains") Crossroads just south of Flint Hill. Flint Hill appears on both modern and Civil War era maps, and Gaines Crossroads shows up in the *Atlas to the Official Records of the War of the Rebellion*.[70] Indeed, the country is hilly, and the route between the mountains is remarkable. Ware and his unit leave the road, which is highly unusual for a marching group of men. Most officers liked to keep their men on the roads: Marching on a road was usually more comfortable for the men, and organization was maintained. Nevertheless, Ware's march probably took him along modern Route 688, which leads from the Salem Road (Route 647) to Markham ("Marcum") Station on the Manassas Gap—now the Southern—Railroad. Another long and tiring day for Ware, with the prospect of more to come.

---

[69] *O.R.*, Vol. 27, Part 2, 747–48. Several other excellent accounts of the cavalry fighting over the mountain passes are available, including Burke Davis's *The Last Cavalier* and John W. Thomason's *Jeb Stuart*.

[70] *Atlas to the O.R.*, Pl. XXII, 5.

Wednesday 17

the rebels are still in Pennsylvania, the people are preparing to meet them as they deserve all quiet in camp Hooker's army is still on the move but its destination unknown to us. the weather is very warm all day rain is very much needed at present health is good in our Regiment and the men are in good spirits.

Franklin Horner

June 17th. "Wednesday." 1863.

Drums beat for all to be up & ready to march at day, without anything scarsly to eat (as we left our old Camp so hastily only cooked part the rations & left part the flour). Herd that Gen'l "Ewell" had surrounded "Millroy" & captured 6000 of his army, commissary stores waggons horses & evry thing & "Millroy" made his escape with a few Cavalry but little fighting done but surrounded at Winchester. This report comes from very reliable source it created great elation among the wearied soldiers. We left at sunrise, left in front Benning's Brig in front the Div & 15th Ga in front the Brig. We marched down the Gap R. R. here all the sick & those unable to march were sent across the Mts a nearer way to "Paris" a village in the Mountains on the pike leading to Winchester, near "Ashby's" Gap. T. Albea & B. Elliott of our Co. were unwell & sent.

We followed the R. R. some distance then crossed going a very rocky & hilly road between the Mt'ns. Water cool & very plentiful, mountains on either side which makes it a beawtiful country. The Timbers all torn up & burnt on the R. R. Some very fine farms & fine dwellings, a few farms in cultivation, lands very rich & was before the war the most beawtiful section of Va.

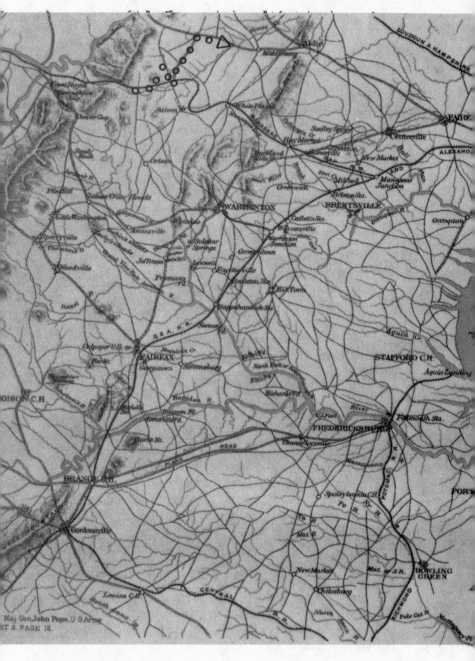

Ware's route, June 17

We marched the "Salem" road untill we came to "Piedmont" Station. At this place Gen'l "Johnson's" army marched the 16th of July & took the cars for Manassas. Here a noble lady presented the Reg'mt with some 2 gal'ns of milk & a large bucket of ham & buisket. Here a great many of the different Brigades had stragled ahead & Gen'l Benning placed them in front with 2 guns & a guard apiece.

At "Piedmont" we took the "Piedmont" Paris & Winchester" turn pike. The road was tolerable good but very long hills & about the hottest day I ever marched, lands very rich & all farms have rock fences. Some very large farms & fine dwellings, very thickly setled, few farms in cultivation.

Several were sunstroke & over 100 of the Reg'mt fell out so much overcome by heat. "Glaze" "Ashmore" P. Norman & W. Tatom quite sick & fell out, some of them placed in Ambulance. Some the "Co" over half the men have fallen out, I never saw men so much fatigued & it was hottest march we ever done. We stopped & rested near "Upperville" & then marched through the beautiful village of Upperville, & then filed right & left the main Winchester pike & took the "Winchester" Paris Fairfax C. H. & Alexandria pike. "Uppervill" is situated on "Winchester" & "Alexandria" pike on a beawtiful eminence, mountains all around. The situation is beawtiful & before the war a fine place the town lies on both sides the pike. Some very fine houses & beawtiful ladies. We stopped at 4 P. M. 1 mile beyond the town & rested 'till sun set, then called in line & marched ½ mile down the road & remained all night. 1 Company from each Reg't of the Brig was sent out on the different roads as pickets. Only "Bennings" Brig came through the village.

A severe Cavalry fight 6 miles below at "Middleburg" the particulars I have not heard.

We had a good nights rest for the first time in 3 nights. Not more than half the Co. for duty, several quite sick from fatigue in Camps & some scattered along the road.

Thomas Ware

Where Horner is getting his information is a mystery. Although the leading elements of the Confederate Army of Northern Virginia are indeed crossing the Potomac into Maryland, they won't be in Pennsylvania for a few more days. What he is describing probably comes from the reports of refugees fleeing Jenkins's Confederate cavalry after the Battle of Winchester. Milroy's wagon train showed up near Chambersburg, Pennsylvania, and the panic caused by their flight was infectious: Farmers, shopkeepers, housewives with their valuables, children, cows, horses, and a large group of black men and women fearing enslavement by the Confederates rushed from the border counties toward Harrisburg and beyond, raising immense clouds of dust in the dry June heat.[71]

Ware, too, reports his side's version of the victory at Winchester, and though the numbers of Union losses are exaggerated, the news buoys the spirits of the bone-weary soldiers on the march.

An on-site examination of the area around Markham, Virginia, shows that it is an almost ideal campsite, with level fields and a stream running through it. Unfortunately, the 15th Georgia's stay there is short. Those disabled by the rigors of the march are sent on a different road so as not to impede the combat troops.

Ware mentions that the 15th Georgia is leading Benning's Brigade, which is leading the division on the march. While this may have been somewhat comforting to the soldiers in that they didn't have to breathe stirred-up dust from the rest of the division marching in front of them, their seemingly random position in the marching column may have had a more important, and unknown, future effect on the individuals in the unit once they went into battle.

Most of the drilling done by soldiers during the Civil War dealt with battlefield maneuvers, wherein the troops were lined up shoulder-to-shoulder, generally in two ranks, and wheeled, advanced, obliqued, and retreated like so many rectangular blocks. Battle tactics devised during the time of the Romans, and refined over the years until Napoleon turned them into an art form, still dictated that soldiers face one another in parallel lines and the attacking force advance until within firing range, fire a

---

[71] Coddington, 149.

volley or two, then rush to drive the enemy from its position.

On the march along narrow roadways, however—in Europe and especially in thickly forested America—the men must be strung out in a column, two or four abreast, and as long as is needed. Special maneuvers were developed for moving the men from the marching column into battlelines quickly and efficiently.

As the separate units in the marching column are ordered, that is usually how they will go into battle should one break out suddenly. Sometimes it seems as if fate chooses certain individuals to fight and die long before they are even aware of the events that are taking place.

Ware mentions following the railroad for a distance. While it would seem that walking along a railroad would provide a level, cleared way, men marching in column generally disliked having to adjust their stride to the distance between ties. Gen. Joshua

"... lands very rich & all farms have rock fences."

Chamberlain, in his classic work *Passing of the Armies*, recalled an attempt he had made to help his men avoid marching in the thick mud that sucked at their feet as they returned home from Appomattox.

> Near Evergreen Station we struck the Southside Railroad, and hoping to save the men's strength, I told the colonel of the leading regiment to have his men take the railroad track and keep out of the heavy mud. They tried it for a while, but soon I saw them jumping back into the mire ankle deep; and, wondering at this, I felt rebuked for my simplicity, when informed that the men found it much more wearing to watch the varying distance of the cross-ties spaced anywhere from eighteen inches to two feet, and measure every step accordingly, than to take the road as it was, and be free to put their feet down wherever they could get them out again. So dear is liberty.[72]

Ware writes, however that the timbers (ties?) were all torn up and burned, so perhaps it wasn't quite as tiring for the short time they were on the railroad.

Piedmont Station (now called Delaplane) was where Confederate general Joseph E. Johnston loaded his troops on a train as they arrived from the Shenandoah Valley so that they could reinforce General P. G. T. Beauregard at Manassas in July of 1861. Apparently, this first instance of moving troops by the ultimate in transportation technology of the day made enough of an impression on Ware and the men around him to warrant his recognizing the small railroad station as historic. And while it is obvious that one lady's efforts at attempting to feed and quench the thirst of more than three hundred men with two gallons of milk and a bucket of ham and biscuits must have been in vain, her generosity is nevertheless recorded for posterity by Thomas Ware of faraway Georgia.

---

[72] Chamberlain, 274–75.

Apparently Ware's brigade commander, General Benning, is having trouble with other commanders' brigades whose stragglers are clogging up his march route. He uses a couple of cannons to persuade them to keep up with their units.

Again, a miserably hot day takes its toll on the soldiers. The only road that goes directly to Upperville from Delaplane and corresponds with Civil War maps is now numbered Route 712. With the exception of macadam, the road remains much as Ware describes it, with lovely old farmhouses and undulating rock fences climbing the long hills that took their toll on the tired men from Georgia, including a large number of Ware's very good friends and one former messmate.

The road Ware marched strikes Upperville at its west end, and since Ware talks of going through the village (and later passing back through it to head for Paris), he must have turned right and marched east, through the town, to camp a mile and a half from Upperville.

Down the road to the east from Upperville, Jeb Stuart is attempting to hold off the prying Union cavalry, who would love to peek through the mountain passes into the Shenandoah Valley and discover where Lee's army is located. There will be a couple more days of cavalry skirmishing as the Northern cavalry attempts to reconnoiter and the Southern horsemen block them. No doubt Ware's unit is sent out toward Middleburg this evening to act as infantry support to Stuart, though Ware, as an infantryman and not a tactician, doesn't realize this.

In spite of modern encroachment from Washington, the village of Upperville, Virginia, has changed little since the Civil War. The old houses have been kept up, and the village in the summer still has the quaint, sultry atmosphere of a place waiting for something to happen. There's a small country church where the road from Piedmont enters Upperville. There's a graveyard there as well, with tombstones predating the Civil War. Ware and the men of the 15th Georgia marched past this church, and perhaps a few of them, Ware included, gazed upon the same worn stones and found their thoughts lingering a little longer than they might have when they were still civilians, as they pondered what could be in store in the near future and what they themselves might leave behind.

Ware's route, June 18

Thursday, June 18, 1863

the war news are more cheering this morning the rebels are leaving Pennsylvania again nothing from the west, very warm to day rainging some this evening all quiet in camp health good nothing new from the seat of war this evening nothing from Hookers army

Franklin Horner

June 18th. "Thursday." 1863.

Very dusty day. Received orders to leave by sun rise which we did; about faced & marched back through the village on the Winchester pike (at Upperville the "Piedmont" pike Joines the "Winchester" & Alexandria pike)

Our aim in coming such a crooked route was to get possession of "Asby's" Gap by coming in at "Upperville" & thus in the rear.

We marched up the pike & soon came to "Paris" a small village in the mountains, the village is old. Here we rested 2 hours, mountains all around & a gradual ascent from the village to the top of the mountain. Excellent water all around, few people living along the road.

We soon passed through the Gap & the scenery was grand, mountains & plains could be seen as far as the eyes would permit & now a descent down to the noted "Shenandoah" which is only 2 miles at the foot of the mountain. Where runs the river is a beawtiful country, fine farms & dwellings, & one of the beawtifulest country to live in I ever saw. Here we crossed the Shenandoah which we waded, it was waist deep & 200 yds wide. Beyond the river & near it is a limestone spring so bold the current a few feet below would turn a mill. Here the cooking detail of the Division were preparing rations & all the sick & those unable to march yesterday were at this noted spring. Water very cool, fine farms & houses around.

We marched 1 mile beyond the river & took up Camp. "Laws & Anderson's" Brig were send down the river to Snicker's ford as guard.

We stopped at 3 P. M. & drew Beef & bread (flour) & no Salt. Marched only 8 miles today.

Heavy rain with thunder & lightning fell this eve & continued slowly most the night. Several quite sick in the Co.

Wrote a letter home.

Thomas Ware

H orner must be reporting the fact that Jenkins's Confederate cavalry, after chasing Milroy's wagon train, returned to the main army. Perhaps the most interesting thing about his entries of the last few days is their immediacy. There is no doubt in Horner's mind that something is happening that will probably affect him very soon. As a native Pennsylvanian with friends and family in the western part of that state, his concerns extend beyond his own role in the army and the potential for becoming engaged in what could become, quite literally, a fight for his own life.

Reading some of the earliest entries in Horner's diary, from July and August 1861, one realizes that there was an attempt made at one time to edit them. He must have paged back through the diary and inserted additional reminiscences, or perhaps added hindsight to some of his early writings. Fortunately, he didn't have the time or the inclination to edit the entire diary, and the later entries remain exactly as he wrote them in the field. Although he occasionally reports rumors as truth (which serve to confirm the entries' authenticity), his impressions as he recorded them through the Gettysburg Campaign segment of his diaries remain unaltered.

After a good night's rest, Ware heads west, passes back through the village of Upperville, and stops in Paris, another tiny settlement along the side of the mountain. As he ascends the Blue Ridge Mountains, he notices the view, which we can still appreciate today. The gap he passes through is called Ashby's Gap, and it was this entryway into the Shenandoah Valley that the Union Cavalry was denied by Jeb Stuart's men.

Ware mentions crossing the Shenandoah River and discovering a limestone spring on the other side, where the cooks and doctors of the division have set up camps. Although a concrete springhouse has been built around it, the spring Ware saw, which supplied the division with fresh water, still flows into the river and can be seen today. It is back in the woods a bit, so with just a little imagination, one can envision ghostly medical men and support personnel moving to and fro, collecting water at the spring and distributing it around the temporary campsite.

Ware marches another mile to camp for the night.

"Here we crossed the 'Shenandoah'."

Ware's route, June 19

Friday 19

cloudy this morning had sevrl heavy rain showers to day the rebels are still in Md but not in heavy force nothing from Hookers army a member of Co G Died to day and was berried this evening Lt Wm Odern returned to the company to day sergt Dick is at little york recruiting

Franklin Horner

June 19th. "Friday." 1863.

Very wet & Cloudy morning. Received orders to leave, soon in lines & left marching a country road down the river. Our object now was to get possession of "Snicker's" Gap on the "Winchester & Leesburg" pike. (As rumors are that "Hooker's" force was marching to get this noted position.) (As we captured a dispatch from "Hooker" to "Stoneman" saying to hold the Gap at all Hazard.) The road from "Ashby's" to "Snicker's" ford was 10 miles, the road very rocky & hilly. We followed the river all the way fine farms & plantations people living finely.

We arrived at the ford at 1 P. M. & again waded the river it was waist deep & 200 yds wide & now a gradual ascent to the top of Blue ridge to the Gap which was 3 miles all pike it was very tiresome marching (all the waggons & baggage was left over the river as a fight was expected, as we heard various rumors from Cavalry.)

Arriving at the top the scenery was sublime & we could with a glass see many miles. This is a strong position as there is only one way for the enemy to come up, & on top 2 pikes comes together, viz. the "Winchester & Leesburg" & "Winchester & Middleburg" pike leading in the main Alexandria pike. At "Middleburg" the village of "Snickersville" is situated at the foot of the Mt.

At this strong position Artillery was placed & here at the fork our Brig stopped to Camp & Division in our rear; the 15th Ga marched on down the pike to "Snickersville" & formed a line in the village which was an old place. The Citizens very much frightened as they expected a fight, several left.

Co" "H" was sent out on picket & the Reg'mt then marched back & joined the Brig. in Camps on the Leesburg pike about 300 yds from the foot of the Mt. a very uneasy position & very rocky to sleep. We placed rock at our feet to hold against & if a rock started to roll it never stopped 'till it reached the foot unless by some larger ones, so none could sleep in our front. The rocks were rolling down all night (I slided down 5 feet from where I first lie by morning).

Heavy cannonading towards Manassas at dark, it commenced raining at 9 P. M. & rained as fast as I ever saw it for 1 hour & then slowly all night. All got very wet & no fire nor wood. I lie down as wet as water could make me & a wet blanket, but got but little sleep being so wet & such an uneasy position. We will long remember that dreadful night.

Thomas Ware

Horner mentions the rain, but being in a fixed camp, it didn't affect him as much as it did Ware, who would be lucky if he had a few tree branches to cover him when he completed his march. The fact that a man in Co. G died of some illness, after two years of war, draws no more of a comment from Horner than the fact that they had rain.

The movements of the 15th Georgia and the brigade it was in make it clear that it was being used as support for the Confederate Cavalry in its role as a screen for the rest of the army. While the main body of the Southern army headed northward and passed to the west of it, Ware's unit was positioned between the invading Confederates and the Union reconnaissance forces east of the Blue Ridge Mountains.

The road Ware took from his campsite on the morning of June

19 along the Shenandoah River to where he crossed to approach Snicker's Gap is remarkable. Modern Route 621 begins as a macadam road heading northeast. As it nears the Shenandoah, it dissolves into a packed dirt and gravel backroad and appears just as it did to Ware and his comrades. For about seven miles it follows the floodplain of the Shenandoah or ribbons up steep hills to leave the river for a while. On a hot June day, with the dust under your feet rising to cling to the sweat on your face and grate in your eyes, it is difficult to tell which century you inhabit.

When a Civil War unit went into camp, it was standard procedure to send out "pickets," who would spread themselves out between the camp and where they thought the enemy was. Their job was to fire at anyone approaching if they couldn't give the proper password. Ware's company had been on picket duty before, and it is not an assignment conducive to getting a good night's sleep.

After dropping off Co. H at its picket post, the rest of the regiment returned to about three hundred yards up the side of the mountain. Ware's description of that night needs no amplification.

"[We] left marching a country road down the river."

Ware's route, June 20

Saturday 20

cool this morning the rebels are still in maryland nothing new from Gen Hookers army cloudy and cool all day quiet in camp furloughs are stoped for the present health good in camp

Franklin Horner

June 20th. "Saturday." 1863.

Still raining slowly, got up early & built fires, & all the fences around & dryed tolerable well. Several the boys went out & bought butter which is very plentiful at 50c.

Orders to leave at 9 A. M. formed a line & marched left in front to the Gap at the fork of the pike & then filed right & marched up the Mt'n which was a gradual ascent for 1 mile when we stoped, joining "Anderson's" Brig which was on the left. So these 2 Brigades occupied 2 miles up the Mt. & "<u>Laws</u> & <u>Roberson's</u>" Brigades on the right, thus the Divi'on holds 4 miles. Each "Co" built their own breast-works of rock 3 feet high which was soon done & trimed out the bushes in front. Artillery was placed in position at the pikes. So now this Div. can hold 10 times their number. Our Regm't is over 1 mile up the Mt; heavy clouds & still raining, very dark. We soon finished our rock works then built fires & rested, still raining. At 3 P. M. orders came to leave immediately. (Our cooking detail was cooking) we marched down the Mt. & in the pike leading to the river; (our rations was not half cooked & we had to carry 2 days rations of beef in our hands & wade the river, our flour was hauled).

The pike was crowded with artillery infantry & waggons going down the Mt'ns; "<u>Pickett's</u>" Divi'on in front. We waded the river (orders not to take off our clothes, few obeyed it) the river was quite deep from the heavy rains. So this makes the 3d time we have crossed the river in 36 hours.

We marched up the pike 1 mile & encamped in a grove at 6 P. M. more than half the Brig had waded the river & was very wet & then stop where there was no wood! The men commenced taking rail but was stopped, but at last the fence was given up & each "Co" pay for what rails they burnt. We soon had large fires & cooked 2 days rations & by 12 P. M. we were dry. We were up half the night cooking &c So I slept but little. Clear & pleasant night. Most the "Co" joined us & now have a very good "Co" most the sick well.

But little sleep by me.

Thomas Ware

While Franklin Horner still waited comfortably in camp, Thomas Ware spent one of the most frustrating and tiring days of his life. First they marched back up the mountain to Snicker's Gap, where they met up with Law's and Robertson's Brigades of Hood's Division. They built breastworks, or field fortifications, which usually consisted of a trench with dirt and rocks piled up and an area in front cleared of trees and brush for a good field of fire. This procedure was all but unknown at the beginning of the war, when the two armies merely faced each other across open fields and blazed away. Though Napoleon's maxim of "Choose your ground, and make the enemy attack you" was known to every officer, by now even the dullest soldier in either army knew that it was better to pick your own place to fight, build something to hide behind, and await the enemy's attack.

After spending most of the day in hard labor constructing the works, Ware's unit began to cook well-deserved rations. Suddenly, with rations half cooked, the order came to head back across the river. Standing at Snicker's Ford, where modern Route 7 crosses the Shenandoah, you can picture the half-naked men balancing muskets, cartridge boxes, blankets, and bundles of clothes, as well as partially cooked meat, over their heads as they made their way across the swollen river.

At the other side, they could find no wood with which to complete their cooking. Needless to say, their mood was less than conciliatory when some commander stopped them from confiscating the only wood available: a farmer's fence. The officer probably knew that he was pleading a lost cause in ordering them not to dismantle the fence. Many methods of preserving civilian fences from becoming government firewood were tried; all failed. The classic example was the order that came down from headquarters saying that only the top rail may be used for firewood. As each unit passed the fences, the men took what they perceived as the top rail, until the fence had completely vanished. Probably the closest anyone could come to satisfying the farmer was what happened with Ware's unit. Even though the farmer was paid in Confederate money, at least he received something for his fence.

The next day was spent by Ware and his unit in much-needed inactivity.

"Marched up the Mt'n which was a gradual ascent for 1 mile ..."

Sunday, June 21, 1863

weather is cloudy and cool all day had Regimental in spection at 8 O clock. about that time heavy firing commenced towards Leesburg and it continues all day our forces and the rebels had a battle it was in our favor nothing from the front yet camp rumors are plenty

Franklin Horner

June 21st. "Sunday." 1863.

Cloudy morning, orders to be ready to leave by sun rise, all up early & drum beat for to form the line & thus we remained some time awaiting orders to march, by 10 A. M. more than half the men were sleep with their baggage & accoutrements on. At 1 P. M. Gen'l "Hood" passed through Camps & told Gen'l "Benning" to pick out a better Camp & have "Co" inspection &c as several had wet ammunition from wading the river. "Benning" remained in the same Camps (no doubt as good as he could find). Inspection over several gone to the river to wash. Dress parade & orders to prepare to move immediately. So by dark all were ready to leave & awaited 'till late. So we unrolled our blankets & soon made a pallet & were to sleep. "Slept finely."

Thomas Ware

What Horner hears from his location southwest of Washington is the cavalry fighting going on along the eastern fringes of Lee's army as it moves up the Shenandoah Valley. There was sharp fighting at Upperville, where Ware had camped on June 18. Though Horner hears that the battle went in the Northern troops' favor, they ultimately failed in their mission, which was to drive through Ashby's Gap and keep an eye on the main body of the invading Confederate Army.

Dress parade for Ware and the Confederates who were on an active campaign was a little different than dress parade for Horner. With no fancy dress uniforms (the Confederates on an invasion traveled extremely light, and all superfluous equipment had been boxed up and sent to Richmond) and many lacking equipment that had been scarce even at the beginning of the war, the most the Confederates could do to prepare for dress parade was brush off the dust from their coated shell jackets, polish gunmetal with wood ashes, and rearrange accoutrements so they at least looked as if they cared about appearance.

In the spring of 1862, Ware had complained that his pack weighed about twenty-five pounds.[73] By now one can assume that his burden is much lighter. The pack is probably gone, with his extra clothing rolled up flat inside his wool blanket. If he had a gum blanket (or rubber poncho), he would have rolled that around his blanket and its contents to keep them dry. He tied the two ends of the rolled blanket together and slipped the light, flexible roll over his head to be slung from shoulder to hip. Confederate soldiers commonly carried their toothbrushes in their buttonholes.[74]

Underneath the slung blanket and over his jacket, Ware carried a haversack, a rough cloth bag hanging from right shoulder to left hip. In his haversack he carried many personal items, such as bits of food and coffee, sugar, writing paper, letters from home, pencil or pen, tin plate, money, eating utensils, pocketknife, guncleaning tools, and, most likely, a twist of tobacco. (Though Ware or Horner never mention smoking or chewing tobacco, we can assume that both indulged: Tobacco was enormously popular and widely accepted in the armies of the Civil War, holding none of the health stigma it does today.) One thing we know Ware carried in his haversack was his precious journal; it could never have been far from his hand.

Nestled underneath his haversack, to keep it in as much shade as could be expected, was Ware's canteen. Going into battle,

---

[73] Ware Diary, April 7, 1862.
[74] Fremantle, 301.

the men would strip themselves of all useless impedimenta—blanket rolls, haversacks, even cartridge boxes, some preferring to carry the cartridges in their pockets—piling everything up behind the lines to remain at the mercy of rear-echelon troops.[75] One thing a soldier never left behind, though it was one of the heaviest pieces of equipment he carried, was his canteen. Every soldier knew that if he was wounded, water could mean the difference between death and survival.

Tied somehow to the canteen, either on the shoulder strap or on the chain or string that held the stopper, was the ubiquitous tin cup. Perhaps the most versatile piece of equipment in both armies, the tin cup was used to brew coffee during the ten-minute rest given every hour on the march, to scoop water from a stream in passing, or to hold huckleberries gathered from a bush just off the march route. Without the tin cup, the armies on the march would have been virtually silent, the mere swishing of brogans in the dust emanating from the column. But the tin cup bumping against the bayonet socket or the canteen or the pocketknife in the haversack, tens of thousands of times over, brought a mechanical, rhythmic, inexorable music to the Civil War that was as recognizable and stirring to the common soldier as "The Battle Hymn of the Republic" or "Dixie."

On his right hip, either slung over his shoulder from left to right or strapped to his waist belt, was his cartridge box. These weighed a couple of pounds on active campaign, when the soldiers were issued forty rounds in preparation for combat.[76] Strapped to Ware's waist belt was a smaller pouch that contained percussion caps. The caps were shaped like tiny top hats and were made out of copper with a dot of fulminated mercury inside. When struck

---

[75] Ware Diary, March 23, 1862: Sometime during the beginning of March, Ware's unit was ordered to carry all tents and extra bags to the Manassas Gap Railroad, presumably to be stored there or shipped; he finds out on March 23 that all the baggage sent to Manassas was burned. Again, in the marching during the Peninsula Campaign in the first weeks of May 1862, they leave their knapsacks on one road and return by another. Ware loses everything, their clothing being taken by another regiment and the rest burned.

[76] Ibid., March 27, 1863. Ware talks about packing his haversack with four days' rations and being issued forty rounds and a blanket in preparation for going into a fight.

by the rifle musket's hammer, they would send a spark into the powder-filled barrel and discharge the projectile at about nine hundred feet per second.

Of course, Ware also carried his weapons. Most likely he carried the particularly cruel-looking triangular bayonet, common to Civil War soldiers, both Union and Confederate. That he ever used it on another human being is doubtful. A careful reading of his earlier existing diary entries does not reveal any time that Ware was in hand-to-hand combat with the enemy. As well, Civil War hospital records indicate that the number of bayonet wounds relative to the number of wounds from small-arms fire was so small as to be insignificant—unless, of course, you were the one who happened to be run through by the cold steel. Some historians have offered theories as to the small number of bayonet wounds: Perhaps the bayonet didn't leave the soldier alive to make it to the hospital and into the records, or perhaps Victorian Era Americans just didn't relish driving the weapon into another human body.

Tactics used during the Revolutionary War dictated that soldiers of the line fire a volley at about fifty to seventy-five yards, then sprint the distance to the enemy and finish him off—including the wounded—with one or more thrusts of the bayonet. When shoulder arms would fire accurately only seventy-five yards, it was easy for attacking troops to march to that point, then rush the enemy and rely on the bayonet to finish the job. The psychological effect upon a defensive line watching a disciplined Redcoat charge vanguarded by burnished steel certainly was telling: Many simply ran.

During the Civil War, a line of attacking infantry would begin to take volleys at three hundred yards—far too great a distance to begin a sprint and have any energy left for fighting. The soldiers would continue to take a volley every thirty seconds or less, as they walked calmly into the maelstrom. Tactically, the emphasis on finishing the job off with the bayonet must have been diminished. Still, we read reports of the singularly military sound, when an attack was being pressed, of hundreds of bayonets being fixed to defenders' rifle muskets and of the long, glittering waves of bayonet-tipped attackers.[77]

---

[77] Ware Diary, May 7, 1862. Ware sees the rare sight of an entire division stretched out in battleline, thirty thousand troops (a bit of an overestimate) with glistening "Bayonetts."

Being a first sergeant, Ware was also entitled to carry a non-commissioned officer's sword. If he ever received one, he never mentions it; if he had one, he probably left it in the company wagon.

The common shoulder arm for infantrymen during the Civil War was the rifle musket, a modern refinement of the standard shoulder arms that had served soldiers since 1611, when King Gustavus Adolphus redesigned the cumbersome Swedish musket to lighten it, added a wheel lock for ignition, then retrained some 65 percent of his pikemen as combat musketeers.[78]

Ware never mentions what type of weapon he carries, but from earlier diary entries we can surmise that it was a rifle musket, a highly refined shoulder weapon every bit as deadly and accurate as anything produced in the twentieth century.[79]

The rifle musket weighed between eight and nine pounds (depending on the manufacture) and was a muzzleloader. A skilled rifleman could load and fire three shots a minute under ideal conditions. Obviously, combat could not be considered ideal conditions, so the rate of fire was considerably slower once the firing started. But though the rate of fire was slow, the accuracy of the weapon was, in the hands of a veteran, superb.

The reason for the rifle musket's accuracy was twofold. First, there was a series of gradually twisting grooves down the inside of the barrel, which imparted a spin on the projectile. The spin gave more distance and a little better accuracy to the lead ball or conical projectile that were used prior to 1849. Then, a Capt. C. E. Minié of the French Army introduced a minor modification to the one-ounce conical projectile that hundreds of thousands of American soldiers would pay royalties on with their blood.[80] The modification was a simple depression in the base of the conical bullet. When the weapon fired, the black powder turned into hot, expanding gases. The gases warmed the soft lead, expanded into the

---

[78] Dyer, 61.

[79] Ware Diary, June 14, 1862. Ware mentions that his unit was specifically chosen to be moved to an area during the fighting on the Peninsula because "we had long range guns." Many Confederates were armed with smoothbore muskets of War of 1812 vintage. Ware's unit obviously was armed with the more modern rifle musket, either the British-made Enfield, a captured Union Springfield, or a Confederate copy.

[80] Nesbitt, 175.

depression, and squeezed the bottom of the bullet into the rifling grooves, making a tight seal. The result was an increase of maximum range from a few hundred yards to nearly a mile. Fighting distances went from less than a hundred yards to three hundred and more. The weapon was accurate as far as a sharp-sighted soldier could see.[81]

Each soldier, then, Yankee or Rebel, was a somewhat self-contained fighting, marching unit, spending most of his time with two or three of his messmates, carrying just enough to sustain himself for two or three days. While the soldiers are aware of being a part of a large mass of men, both on the march and eventually in battle, their vision and experiences are limited to those immediately surrounding them and grow even more limited once they are in a great battle.

---

[81] Brig. Gen. Stephen Weed was mortally wounded on Little Round Top and Lt. Charles Hazlett shot dead across his body on July 2, 1863, at Gettysburg. The nearest Confederates were in Devil's Den, triangulated at a little more than five hundred yards from the rock where Weed and Hazlett fell. Maj. Gen. John F. Reynolds, according to Glenn Tucker in *Lee and Longstreet at Gettysburg* (214), was killed the day before by a Confederate at eight hundred yards, and Tucker writes that Maj. Gen. John Sedgwick was killed at Spotsylvania at a similar distance (ibid., 100).

Ware's route, June 22

Monday 22

all quiet this morning we put a floor in our tent and then go and get a many cherries as we can eat. A circular was read on Dress parade this evening that our forces were victorious yesterday and captured a great many prisoners and arms and drove the rebels seven miles through Ashby's gap all quiet this evening

Franklin Horner

June 22nd. "Monday." 1863.

Beawtiful morning. Received orders to leave at 6 A. M. Soon all ready the supposition is we are going to cross the river. We left at the time crossing the pike & marched the same road up the river towards the "<u>Alexandria</u>" pike the same way we came a few days ago. As report says that the enemy are making an atemp to attack. So only 3 Brigades went leaving "<u>Anderson's</u>" at "<u>Snicker's</u>" Gap to guard it. We arrived at the pike near the ford at 12 A. M. & rested in a grove 2 hours. <u>Mc"Laws"</u> Division was guarding this point (viz "<u>Ashby's</u>" Gap) the enemy drove our Cavalry to the Gap & captured a great many, they seeing we had infantry here they fell back; we expected a fight in the eve. But no go. (It is supposed they are making a feint here to draw our attention. A few days will develop & we will see) So the 3 Brigades left the ford marching up the pike towards "<u>Winchester</u>" marched 4 miles & encamped at a village called "<u>Millwood</u>" at 5 P. M. & drew 2 days rations & cooked, we were up late cooking, no salt, lard or soda. Slept very well Water some distance.

Thomas Ware

Still Horner is enjoying the comforts of camp life. One of his messmates has apparently found some finished wood, so they could afford the luxury of a floor inside their tent. Unfortunately, they will be able to enjoy it for only a few more days.

The fighting for Ashby's Gap—which has occupied a good bit of Horner's writing time and has added an extra forty miles to Ware's march—is over. While Horner states, apparently from an official Union circular, that their forces drove the Confederates through the Gap, this is not true. The series of battles fought by Stuart through Aldie, Middleburg, and Upperville were classic holding actions against a much larger force. Jeb Stuart was aided by his outstanding—but dwindling—group of subordinate officers, whom he let control their own units' actions more than ever before.

Still, even though Horner's interpretation of the circular says the Union was victorious, they failed to drive the Southern Cavalry back far enough to determine the location of the main army. By now, the tail of it has passed and the Union Cavalry has missed its chance.

The fighting was severe due in part to the funneling nature of the mountains in the area. The Union attackers lost about eight hundred killed, wounded, and missing; the Confederates had about five hundred removed from the active list.[82]

Because of the action along the Alexandria Pike (where Aldie, Middleburg, and Upperville are situated), Ware was ordered to return from Snicker's Gap to back up the cavalry. His campsite was near a small village called Millwood, the site of Carter Hall, Stonewall Jackson's Headquarters for a few days in November of 1862.[83]

---

[82] Davis, 320.
[83] Schildt, 82.

Tuesday 23

weather cool this morning nothing from the front to day, get orders to be ready to march at a moments notice with three days rations in Haversacks we pack our coats in boxes ready to leave so now wer are ready to march at moments notice we know not where camp rumor dont agree on the course health good

Franklin Horner

June 23d. "Tuesday." 1863.

Pleasant morning, all up early expecting to leave. Waggons passing by, roads crowded. Still in Camps at 9 A.M. the boys lying about resting & expecting a hard march before night.

10 A.M. received orders to wash & clean up & rest today. Considerable rejoicing in the Brig. as all were very glad as we needed it. Several gone out foraging, but got but little. Inspection at 5 P. M. But little wood about Camps & water very scarce; night has come

Received orders to leave before day tomorrow. Orders read to us tonight relative to marching. No stragling, no pressing private property evry man keep his place as we are going in M'd. We cooked beef tonight without salt, & now have 3 days of bread & 1 of Beef & no salt.

Beawtiful night, lie down early to be ready for tomorrows march.

Thomas Ware

I t is difficult to imagine the anticipation in Horner's camp as they receive orders to prepare to march. Any rumors contrary to those saying they will be after Lee's invading army are just wishful thinking. The men with Horner, who had been put on this special assignment as reserve troops, now realized the gravity of the invasion. Certainly Horner feels that same nervous fluttering in his stomach as he had before fighting on the Virginia Peninsula or just before Antietam.

Horner had seen combat before. On June 26, 1862, he came under hostile fire for the first time: "the company came in from picket this morning at two O clock hear some firing to our right three O P. M. heard musketry got into rifle pits [illegible] O the firing becomes general Shot are flying thick along our heads." And again on the next day when the battle was renewed: ". . . about four O clock, our men fired first they then gave us a volley and we returned it. we then got orders to fall back. we marched back about two miles when we formed a new line where we fought all day, our loss was heavy in Killed and wounded."[84] Again, on August 28, 1862, just before the Second Battle of Manassas, he records, "got into line at three O clock A. M. marched about five mile when our advance was fired into and three men wounded and one killed." In his entries on August 29 and 30, he mentions the battle and the heavy losses they sustained as well as their retreat back to Centerville.

Antietam, for Horner, was a series of battles through the South Mountains of Maryland (September 14, 1862: the Division "stormed the mountain" and had at least two wounded and two killed)[85] and, of course, the horror of their advance through the cornfield early on the morning of September 17, 1862. Sometime between 7:00 and 7:30 A.M. David C. Overdorff, with whom Horner had joined the army on July 24, 1861, was killed. Interestingly enough, in Horner's war records, there are two casualty sheets—one dated "4-4-[18]78" and the other "3-9-[18]82"—that state that Horner had been wounded at the Battle of Antietam, the information having come from casualty lists dated November 2, 1862, from Headquarters, First Army Corps and signed by Gen. John F. Reynolds. In addition, there is a document from the War Department Record and Pension Division that indicates he was

[84] Horner Diary, June 26–27, 1862.
[85] Bates, Vol. I, 901–3.

wounded at the Battle of Antietam. Nowhere else does this show up, including his own diary entries for the dates after the battle.[86]

On September 19, however, Horner records that they "marched about three miles went through the battlefield the dead are laying thick all over the battlefield and are becoming decomposed we encamped in a field for the night and [illegible] our tent. I am not well." On September 21 he writes, "I can scrsely walk," and then reported to the Division as being not fit for duty. On September 23 he reports that his health is good, but a week later, his September 30 entry, in a wavy handwriting, says, "I am not very well to day make out my monthly returns have some trouble getting it right." Perhaps Horner's wound was so slight that he decided to dress it himself, then suffered from the effects of infection—perhaps compounded by some disease contracted because of his proximity to the corpses two days after the battle—for the next two or three weeks until he was finally treated for his wound.

But the most costly battle for Horner's company was fought at Fredericksburg, Virginia, on December 13, 1862: "got into line and marched to the left got in line of battle was not long til we were ordered to charge which we did across a field our loss heavy. Capt Bolar wounded, 3 of our company killed, 11 wounded 5 missing the battle was very severe all the afternoon lasted til dark Gen Jackson and his A[djutant] General were killed [this turned out to be merely a rumor], men are in good spirits what are left of them."

Records support the fact that Capt. Andrew Bolar of Co. H was wounded and captured at Fredericksburg, but that eight of the company were either killed or wounded during the fight.[87]

By March 10, 1863, Horner was at Falls Church, Virginia, and was stationed in Washington when the next great battle—Chancellorsville, May 1–4, 1863—was fought a few miles west of Fredericksburg. According to Samuel Bates's *Martial Deeds of Pennsylvania*, after the division to which Horner's unit was attached had been "reduced to a mere skeleton" and ordered to Washington in February 1863, "The Third Brigade [which in-

---

[86] Military Service Records, National Archives, Franklin Horner File.

[87] Bates, Vol. I, 901–3.

cluded Horner's unit] has its camp near Minor's Hill, and performed picket duty. . . . In April the brigade was ordered to report to General Martindale, in the city of Washington, to perform provost duty, where it remained six weeks."[88]

While he and the men of the 12th Pennsylvania heard conflicting rumors about the results of Chancellorsville, including one that all troops in and around Washington would join General Hooker and the army, they remained in the Washington area until now.

Suddenly the same orders Ware received two weeks earlier now stir Horner's friends: Pack all nonessentials in boxes for shipment to the Capital; draw three days' marching rations; fill haversacks; and be prepared to leave at any time.

Ware and the 15th Georgia enjoy a day of inactivity, other than cooking and washing. He mentions receiving orders concerning the troops' conduct on the invasion; they came directly from Robert E. Lee and yet angered some of those in Richmond over their leniency in light of the type of war the Union forces have carried on in the South.[89]

In short, Lee's General Orders No. 72 protected private property of the civilians; they appointed only certain officers to requisition necessary supplies from local authorities and instructed them to pay market price for those items; and they gave general guidelines on how to handle civilians who refused payment or concealed supplies necessary for the army. In all, they were lenient to the extreme. They were not always adhered to, however, as Ware was to witness soon enough, and so Lee would have to issue stricter orders on June 27.

---

[88] Bates, Vol. I, 885.
[89] *O.R.*, Vol. 27, Part 3, 912–13.

Wednesday June 24, 1863

Warm and pleasant this morning get up rather late Our clothing sent away taken to Washington by the Qr. Mr. nothing from the front the rebels are still in Penna we expect to march soon all quiet in camp health good had a letter from home they are all well [illegible] excitement about the invation

Franklin Horner

June 24th. "Wednesday." 1863.

Drums beat at 2 A.M. for all to be up & ready to march. All up and ready so at the break of day all left, marching left in front marching the "<u>Harpers Ferry</u>" & "<u>Charlestown</u>" turn pike intersecting with the "<u>Alexandria</u> & <u>Winchester</u>" pike at "<u>Millwood</u>". After a march of 6 miles we came to "<u>Berryville</u>" C. H. ("<u>Clark</u>" Co) & rested in the edge of town in rear of the enemies breastworks in their old Camp (here we joined "<u>Anderson's</u>" Brig which we had left the day before guarding Snickers Gap) rested 1½ hour & I got my breakfast at a private house, I was very hungry. (I had plenty of buiskets made without lard soda or salt, & beef too without the latter, which was not pleasant eating)

We marched through town with music crossing the "<u>Leesburg</u>" & "<u>Winchester</u>" pike here, this is an old town few fine buildings & since the enemy has encamped around it, the out houses & fences & yards are ruined & fences burnt. We marched 1½ mile & left the "<u>Harpers Ferry</u>" pike & marched the "<u>Shepardstown</u>" pike for 8 miles. This is a very rich country, a great many citizens left, few farms in cultivation, large fields of wheat. A great many girls out to see us pass. We stopped to rest 2 hours at "Summer point" Station on the "<u>Harpers</u> Farry" & Winchester" R. R. 10 miles from the latter.

Ware's route, June 24

Here we left the pike & marched through plantations & then in a country road very rocky & thinly setled setlement, plenty of water. Marched 4 miles from the Station & came in "Harpers Ferry" & "Bunker Hill" Turnpike at the village of "Middleway". We did not march through the village. A large crowd of girls came out to see us & waved their hand-kerchiefs, we passed them with music.

After a march of 2 miles we crossed "Opequan" Creek a very large stream & 2 miles brought us to Camp in a large piece of woods, at 5 P. M. no water near & all very tired. We drew beef & bought some flour very cheap (as our bread was out) It was 11 P. M. before many of us went to sleep hav-ing marched 18 miles & encamped in "Jefferson" Co. Quite a poor & thinly setled country, houses in ruins few farms in cultivation, lands quite rich. This portion of Va. is about ruined fences all burnt.

Orders to leave at day break.

Thomas Ware

There is a famous quote about the military that could have been coined just as easily in the ranks of the Roman Legions as in the armies of the 1990s: "Hurry up and wait." This is exactly what is happening to Franklin Horner. It had happened to Thomas Ware, too, during the last few weeks. It will happen to both of them again, even though they are on an active campaign and in search of the enemy. The pressure is harder on Horner than Ware, for at least Ware is on the move, with the petty concerns of the march to distract him from the potentially deadly situation he is facing.

Ware is lucky enough to get breakfast at a private home, an unusually pleasant treat for soldiers. In the past, when Ware was in Virginia, he frequently would be invited to a home-cooked meal or perhaps to spend the night in a warm, soft featherbed.[90] But as

---

[90] Ware Diary, February 12, 1862: "I & Corp'l Parks detailed as picket guards to go near Manassas. . . . Eat supper with Miss Jennie Evans & slept for the first time in 7 months on a feather bed; sit up & talk quite late. Moon shone beawtiful." Ware was given dinner by civilians at least two or three more times in March 1862 and numer-ous other times that year while camped in one area for any length of time.

the war continued, civilians in the South had problems feeding even their own families. The home where Ware ate breakfast had apparently been feeling the hardships of war. Perhaps the passing of advance units of the Confederate Army had left his hostess without lard, soda, or salt.

The section of the country the 15th Georgia marches through had seen the passing of armed men before. In September 1862, less than a year before, the Confederate Army had marched this way on their first invasion of the North. That invasion ended in the Battle of Antietam (or Sharpsburg, as it was known to the Southerners), with the Confederates turned back. Perhaps some of the men remembered their march to Sharpsburg.

Part of General Toombs's Georgia brigade played an important role in the Battle of Sharpsburg by manning pits overlooking "Burnside's Bridge" and holding off the Union advance there for several hours with their deadly, accurate fire. The men of the 15th Georgia were held in reserve but had to advance after the rifle pits were abandoned and Burnside's men had moved forward. Ware's regimental commander, Col. W. T. Millican, was killed.[91] More than one of Ware's fellow soldiers remembers the bitter sting of having to turn back into Virginia and the personal, wrenching heartache of losing a friend in battle. Both are feelings that the men hope will not be repeated.

Once again, Ware's memory for details of the march is very helpful in reconstructing his route. (It almost seems as if Ware were taking notes as he marched along. Likely he kept his journal close at hand and during each halt—usually ten minutes' rest for every hour on the march—would take it out and write a little.)

At daybreak they marched along what is now Route 256 in Clarke County, Virginia, from Millwood north to Berryville, there crossing Route 7, the Leesburg and Winchester Pike. (Route 256 becomes modern State Route 340 a few miles north of Millwood, and 340 is the direct road to both Harper's Ferry and Charlestown.) Ware notes the destruction left by the Union Army after it camped here. He and the rest of the army must feel some helpless anger, especially in light of General Lee's General Orders No. 72.

---

[91] Murfin, 283, 362.

Ware writes that he ends up at "Summer Point." The town is identified as Summit Point on both modern maps and the *Atlas to the Official Records*. An irony of war: When Ware camped a mile west of Snicker's Ford on June 20 and 21, he was only four miles from Berryville. Military exigencies demanded his return to Ashby's Gap and Millwood, then an early morning march to get just four miles from where he had been.

At this point we lose Ware's march route. The men of the 15th Georgia wind up marching through what Ware calls, from his Southern upbringing, "plantations."[92] Crossing farm fields, the men end up in the village of Middleway, then cross Opequon Creek. Frustratingly, after having marched eighteen miles, there is no water near the campsite, and they have to purchase flour since the army cannot supply it. Again Ware observes the devastation war has brought upon the countryside.

Not many of us today have ever built a rail fence around a dozen acres or raised fifteen or twenty pigs, feeding them, caring for them, until they were ready for market—or our own frying pan. Few of us have stumbled through a furrow behind a plow pulled by a couple of mules, then planted row upon row of crops; or sown wheat and scythed, sent it to the mill to have it turned into flour (paying the miller for his work, of course), then stored it for the winter. So it is hard to imagine what it is like to have several months of hard, back-bending work digging post holes and splitting rails for fences obliterated in a matter of minutes when a regiment of infantry turns a farm into a campsite. Pigs vanish, flour disappears, and a regiment in double battleline, shoulder-to-shoulder, moving across a field of wheat, tramples it flat in one pass. So when Ware writes about crossing "plantations" or burning fence rails, there is more to it than appears.

---

[92] Reading Ware's detailed routes leads me to believe that Civil War armies abandoned main roads more often than I had previously thought. One reads so often about marches being held up on account of other troops or wagons on the road ahead that one gets the impression the officers attempted to march only on improved roads. Apparently—at least in the Gettysburg Campaign and in Ware's unit—the soldiers left the roads more often than is recorded in the official reports.

June 25

○ ○ ○ *Ware's route*   ● ● ● *Horner's route*

Thursday 25

weather pleasant this morning got orders to march at two P. M. we went as far as Balls cross roads where we halted for the night rained some boys all in good health and spirits we can not tell where we are to go yet however I think we are to join the army of the Potomac till Lee's army is driven to Virginia again.

Franklin Horner

June 25th. "Thursday." 1863.

Cloudy day, apperance of a splendid day to march. Drum beat for all to be up at day & we were in lines in a few moments after. We marched the Bunker Hill pike a short distance. (The latter pike intersecting with the "Winchester & Martinsburg" pike at "Bunker Hill") & then marched a country road for 3 miles & came in the above pike but only marched it for 1 mile. As we came in the pike we came up with our waggons & Baggage train & artillery both the latter marched the pike to "Martinsburg". We filed to the left & marched a rough rocky country road & soon came in "Berkley" Co. Marching paralel with the pike near "Martinsburg" we stopped to rest in the Suberbs of the town we did not march through the place. The town seems as large as Washington. We crossed the "Baltimore & Ohio" R. R. here the depot &c around was burnt, tearing up the track for some distance.

We marched a country road for 2 miles & came in the Martinsburg & Williamsport turn pike. We marched 6 miles from "M" & encamped at 5 P. M. it drizling rain, having marched 21 miles the men were very tired & had to cook 1 days rations of beef. Raining slowly most the night.

Thomas Ware

Though they march less than two miles, finally Horner and his unit have begun to move. His intuition tells him that they are about to join the Army of the Potomac and eventually fight Lee's Army of Northern Virginia. On both counts he is right. Horner seems positive that they will fight until Lee's army is driven back into Virginia. That remains to be seen.

Because it is cloudy, Ware, already having the wisdom of an old campaigner, regards this as a pleasant day to march. From their campsite about two miles from the Opequon, they march the Bunker Hill pike (modern Route 26) and take a country road northward. There is a trace road just to the east of Bunker Hill and a "short distance" from where they had camped the previous night (Route 51/6). It eventually intersects with Route 11, the Old Valley Turnpike, the main road down the Shenandoah Valley, which armies used time and again throughout the war. Once again we lose Ware's line of march: The artillery and wagons take the Valley Turnpike, a well-worn road, suitable for wheeled traffic. The footsoldiers of the 15th Georgia and the rest of the division are sent a rougher road. (There is a road on the *Atlas to the Official Records* map, Pl. XLV, 2., that corresponds roughly to county Routes 30 and then 45, parallels Route 11, and ends up south of Martinsburg crossing the railroad tracks.)

Ware doesn't say whether it was the men of the 15th Georgia who tore up the track and burned the Baltimore & Ohio depot at Martinsburg or some Confederates who passed through earlier. The area they are passing through had been part of Virginia just a week earlier, but on June 20 became the new state of West Virginia by presidential proclamation. Though Thomas Ware doesn't mention it, and may not even realize it, he is now on Union soil.

Bypassing Martinsburg, they again take some country roads but eventually strike the Valley Turnpike again. If Ware and his comrades had been employed tearing up rails and ties, then marched another eight miles, it was indeed a tiresome day.

Friday 26

slept well last night starded this morning at five and half Oclock marched past Drainesville and past the sixth army corps. the boys were geting too tired too march so we encamped at four P. M. till morning in a meddow raining some the are geting very mudy got orders to march at five in the morning nothing from the front to day

Franklin Horner

June 26th. "Friday." 1863.

Drum beat for all to be up & ready to leave by light, raining slowly. We were up early But did not leave 'till Sunrise. We marched the pike which was very slopy & 4 miles we came to the river, none were permitted to strip But plunged the river it was little over knee deep & 200 yds wide (it still raining & we were very wet any way)

We stopped a few moments on M'd side & then left crossing the "<u>Cheesapeak</u> & <u>Washington</u>" Canal & came in <u>Williamsport</u> an old town. At this place the pikes cross the "Martinsburg & <u>Hagerstown</u>" (M. D.) pike & Frederick City (M. D.) & <u>Greencastle</u> Penn pike. We marched the former pike 2 miles & stopped in a grove 2 hours awaiting farther orders & all to get a dram as it was still raining & all were very wet. Several the boys got quite drunk & we had a jolly set.

We soon left leaving the pike & marching a rough mudy country road 2 miles & came into "Williamsport" & "<u>Greencastle</u>" <u>Pen</u> pike at "<u>Chickagig</u>" Creek. Several the <u>Div</u> was quite Jolly & some pass traveling & a few fights, road very good, fine plantations, people very thickly setled, fine crops of wheat & corn. Water good people mostly Union. 7 miles brought us to M. D. & <u>Pen</u> line. People here

June 26

∘ ∘ ∘ *Ware's route*   ● ● ● *Horner's route*

("Franklin" Co) all living well, have plenty to live on & a great many young people in the country. All do their own work.

We stoped to Camp at sun set, marched 16 miles, & up half the night cooking.

We got a great many cherries & living finely.

Thomas Ware

For a week and a half while Ware marched, Horner and his comrades remained in camp. After digging entrenchments, Horner must try out some new muscles as the men begin their march to catch up with Lee's invaders. Within the next few days, these men—who had been assigned noncombat duty because they had already seen the worst of combat—are pulled into the whirlpool created by the Confederates' invasion of the North.

Horner's route takes him from Ball's Crossroads at the intersection of the Leesburg-Alexandria Pike and the road from Falls

"We stopped a few moments on M'd side & then left crossing the 'Cheesapeak & Washington' Canal."

Church to Georgetown, north toward Leesburg. Dranesville is on the Leesburg Pike (modern State Route 7), and they march beyond the town and encamp, too tired to march any farther after about fifteen miles of marching.

This is to be a momentous day for Ware: He will cross the Potomac River, traverse the small "panhandle" area of Maryland, then cross the Maryland line into Pennsylvania. Ware, in one day, is in three states and probably moves farther north than he has ever been in his life.

He marches the Valley Turnpike (U.S. 11) four miles until reaching the Potomac. (This also gives us a good idea where he camped the night before. Four miles south of the river would place his campsite at about the point where the Potomac makes a bend and comes closest to the Valley Turnpike—an ideal place, with plenty of water, for the men to camp.) Crossing the Potomac and stopping on the other side to wring out socks and empty shoes of river water, they bisect the Chesapeake and Ohio Canal.

The C&O Canal (mistakenly called the "Cheesapeak & Washington Canal" by Ware) was, even during the Civil War, a dying mode of transportation. The C&O Canal was originally designed and built in the early nineteenth century to haul passengers and freight to cities and villages along its 184.5 mile length, which paralleled the Potomac River.[93] Shortly after its completion, the railroads began their expansion, moving goods and people at ever-increasing speeds, sometimes approaching thirty or forty miles per hour! Clearly, the plodding mules that pulled the canal boats from their towpaths could not keep up with the technological advances, and the canal gradually fell into financial decline, with the locks breaking down, the small villages that served the passengers being abandoned, and the canal itself running dry in many places. Many of the ferries and fords across which the goods were transported to reach the canal remained in use, however. The towpath was often used by the military as a road, and the canal itself, at least from Poolesville, Maryland, to Washington, was used occasionally to transport pontoons for military bridges.[94] Since it

---

[93] Hahn, 7.
[94] *O.R.*, Vol. 27, Part 3, 354.

parallels the Potomac, every time a body of soldiers crossed the river, even though they don't mention it, they cross the C&O Canal as well.

For the past ten days, the citizens of Williamsport had been seeing the invading Confederates pass in and around their town, beginning with Jenkins's troopers in pursuit of Milroy's trains. Neither Ware nor Horner mentions it, but they may have heard that the Confederate troops were spreading out like a large fan, moving toward Harrisburg, the capital of Pennsylvania, and York, on the road to Philadelphia. In fact, this very day, Confederate general Jubal Early's men pass through one of a number of small Pennsylvania towns they were to capture, demanding 60 barrels of flour, 7,000 pounds of bacon, 1,200 pounds of sugar, 600 pounds of coffee, 1,000 pounds of salt, 40 bushels of onions, 1,000 pairs of shoes, and 500 hats. "The quantities required are far beyond that in our possession," was the worried reply given by David Kendlehart, president of town council of the Borough of Gettysburg.[95]

During their two-hour break after crossing the Potomac, the men actually receive a ration of whiskey. Thought to be a stimulant in the Civil War era, it at least got some of them lively enough to stave off the chill of the rainy day and to elicit a note in Ware's diary.

From where they took their "dram" two miles above Williamsport (on modern U.S. Route 11, what Ware calls the "Martinsburg & Hagerstown pike"), they once again cut cross-country to the Williamsport and Greencastle (Pennsylvania) pike (modern State Route 63). They strike the road at one of the branches of Conococheague Creek (which Ware remembers—not surprisingly—as "Chickagig"). Apparently the "dram" acted as more of a stimulant to some than to others, making them not only jolly, but perhaps a little belligerent as well.

With the farmer's eye for crops, Ware notices how little the war has affected this section of northern Maryland and southern Pennsylvania. After a relatively light day of marching, an early halt, and a raid on a nearby cherry orchard, the simple pleasures of a soldier are reflected in his last observation for the day.

---

[95] From the original Early demand note, owned by John Kendlehart, descendant of David, Gettysburg, Pennsylvania. Quoted from an article in the *Gettysburg Times*, June 29, 1991.

The Gettysburg Campaign, the great Confederate invasion of Pennsylvania, which is to bring a new independent nation into the world and about which millions of words will be written, draws but a few lines from Ware and Horner.

Saturday, June 27, 1863

took up the line of march at six O clock this morning crossed the Potomac at edwards ferry then went as far as the mouth of the monocacy where we encamped about four O clock for the night marched about fifteen miles rained a little nearly all day the boys in good spirits nothing from the front

Franklin Horner

June 27. "Saturday." 1863.

Received orders to leave at 8 A.M. Cool & pleasant day. 15th Ga in the rear. Soon in the pike & then we stopped for 2 hours & several the Q Masters & Sergn'ts armed went ahead with the Pioneers

3 miles then brought us to the beawtiful town of "Greencastle" on the "Harrisburg" R. R. this is a fine town larger than Washington Ga houses large & fine, shady streets. This town like others in this State have never felt the affect of war. The R. R. runs down Main Street. People strong Unionist & looked mad & sullen at our apperance a great many closed doors; stores all closed the Streets & Hotels crowded with young men just out of service. Some nice looking girls dressed very fine as evry thing is cheap. Several Federal Flags were seen the girls had them on their bonnets.

We marched through quick time with music. The Depot on the north side of town was burnt & R. R. in several places.

After leaving town we had the plain mud road to march, very mudy, but we marched through fields of wheat & corn tearing down fences & not respecting scarsly any thing. The soldiers hardly respecting any thing, robing bee gums

June 27
○ ○ ○ Ware's route ● ● ● Horner's route

& poultry yards. We were gathering up all the horses &
beeves in the country. People all very much frightened
along the road; people very thickly setled, cultivate small
farms & live well. Their farms are laid of in squares from
6 to 20 acres, & not even a stump to be seen. Woodland very
scarse.

12 miles brought us to the town of "<u>Chambersburg</u>" this
is as large as "<u>Atlanta</u>" Ga & as nice & fine a town as I ever
saw. This place like the last place has never felt the affect of
war the R. R. passes by, houses large & fine, some the finest
I ever saw. Stores all closed & a great many people out to
see us & looked frightened & mad. The place has 2 very
large & fine Hotels all crowded with citizens & young men
dressed up & all just out of service. So the country & towns
are full of young men not in service, no militia gone from
this place. I saw more girls than I have seen at any one time
before, some very good looking ones. The town under martial law, guards at evry corner, so we could get nothing. The
town is near 2 miles long, some very fine buildings in the
Suberbs of town.

We marched 3 miles from the town & left the road,
marched through a large corn field 1 miles & encamped in a
grove having marched 17 miles. We burnt all the fences
around the corn fields, & waggons & horses in the wheat &
corn field, it was dark when we stopped. Several the boys
gone out in the country (as evry thing is plentiful)

Thomas Ware

Franklin Horner crosses the Potomac River about fifty-five
miles south of where Thomas Ware crossed it yesterday. He
is in pursuit now of Lee's army and with it, though he
doesn't know it, Thomas Ware.

Horner, for some reason, is not as detailed in his descriptions
of his march route as Ware is. Perhaps being so far away from
home is more of an adventure for Ware; perhaps Horner is too
busy or too tired to record events in detail. Earlier entries in
Horner's diary—in 1861 and 1862—are as detailed as Ware's

entries. Maybe his capture at Cold Harbor and wounding at Antietam have jaded his desire to record and remember his later war experiences. Nevertheless, while we cannot follow Horner's exact route, we can determine where he crossed the Potomac and where he camped that night.

Horner and the men of the 12th Pennsylvania Reserves crossed the Potomac on pontoon bridges placed at Edwards Ferry by the engineers.[96] Edwards Ferry today, like most of the crossings on the Potomac called "ferry," no longer has an active ferry boat taking passengers and goods across the Potomac. But ruins from the buildings at the C&O Canal where the old ferry landed are still standing. Horner marched past these buildings and took one of several roads northward, either along the river or across the land made by the broad loop of the Potomac. Eventually he camps where the Monocacy River empties into the Potomac, a broad, flat floodplain that would make an excellent campsite.

Ware gets a little extra time this morning to prepare for the march. The pioneers went ahead of the column to ensure that there would be no delays due to guerrilla activities, such as the felling of large trees across the road or the burning of bridges. Quartermasters advanced to requisition needed supplies from the Northern towns they were about to enter. Armed sergeants (and probably a few other armed men of lesser rank) went along to discourage "bushwhackers" from attempting to snipe at the pioneers and quartermasters, and to encourage cooperation among the town officials.

Now the Southern host is unleashed. In spite of Lee's General Orders No. 72, the men of the Confederacy begin to feast on an amazing abundance unspoiled despite two years of war. Some of the pillaging is in line with military needs, such as the gathering of horses and cattle. But private beehives and chicken houses are clearly being used by the individual soldiers for private consumption. No doubt it was the soldiers' actions outside of Greencastle that prompted the Confederate Army to declare Chambersburg under martial law and post guards about town. As well, it may have been the actions of Ware and the rest of Hood's Division that

---

[96] *O.R.*, Vol. 27, Part 3, 334, 349, 353–54.

". . . went as far as the mouth of the monocacy where we encamped."

caused General Lee to issue General Orders No. 73 from his headquarters in Chambersburg on June 27, 1863. As if he is a father
gently scolding a spirited child he needs to punish but not break,
there is praise as well as stern admonishment in his orders:

> The commanding general has observed with
> marked satisfaction the conduct of the troops on the
> march, and confidently anticipates results commen-
> surate with the high spirit they have manifested.
>
> No troops could have displayed greater forti-
> tude or better performed the arduous marches of the
> past ten days.
>
> Their conduct in other respects has, with few
> exceptions, been in keeping with their character as
> soldiers, and entitles them to approbation and praise.
>
> There have, however, been instances of forget-
> fulness, on the part of some, that they have in keep-
> ing the yet unsullied reputation of the army, and that

the duties exacted of us by civilization and Christianity are not less obligatory in the country of the enemy than in our own.

The commanding general considers that no greater disgrace could befall the army, and through it our whole people, than the perpetration of the barbarous outrages upon the unarmed and defenseless and the wanton destruction of private property, that have marked the course of the enemy in our own country.

Such proceedings not only degrade the perpetrators and all connected with them, but are subversive of the discipline and efficiency of the army, and destructive of the ends of our present movement.

It must be remembered that we make war only upon armed men, and that we cannot take vengeance for the wrongs our people have suffered without lowering ourselves in the eyes of all whose abhorrence has been excited by the atrocities of our enemies, and offending against Him to whom vengeance belongeth, with whose favor and support our efforts must all prove in vain.

The commanding general therefore earnestly exhorts the troops to abstain with most scrupulous care from unnecessary or wanton injury to private property, and he enjoins upon all officers to arrest and bring to summary punishment all who shall in any way offend against the orders on this subject.[97]

On all levels, from great nations to innocent individuals, war is, unequivocally, the cruelest and most hideous aberration of man. Throughout these orders, however, rings the spirit of Robert E. Lee. Regardless of how horrible war could be—and he had seen it as a soldier for more than half his life—Robert E. Lee would make it, by sheer power of personality and influence, as civilized

---

[97] *O.R.*, Vol. 27, part 3, 942-43.

". . . crossed the Potomac at edwards ferry."

as it could be made. Yet wars, in spite of all that can be done, suddenly take on a life and wicked momentum all their own.

During his march through Greencastle and Chambersburg, Ware describes his first real taste of anti-Southern sentiment; yet with the powers of observation capable only of a young soldier far from home, he still manages to notice the pretty women in both enemy towns.

He also manages to compare the towns with some he knows back in Georgia. It seems the farther away from the South Ware gets, the more he begins to think of home. Earlier entries have him reminiscing poignantly. In December 1861, less than five months after he enlisted and ten days before Christmas, he writes in his diary about, "Happy hours I had spent on such a night with one who was far, far from me." In January of 1862, "<u>A. B. C.</u>" his coded sweetheart, invades even his subconscious: "had a pleasant <u>dream</u> of a <u>sertain one</u>." While Ware may mention the pretty girls in northern towns, without a doubt there is just one back home on his mind.

Sunday 28

Took up the line of march at six O clock and crossed the monocacy and marched through Buckstown and joined the fifth army corps where we encamped about one P.M. the weather was pleasant all day we marched about fifteen mile through fine wheat country the wheat is ready to harvest

Franklin Horner

June 28th. "Sunday." 1863.

Apperance of rain. We will remain in Camps today, passes granted & a great many the boys out foraging, the soldiers are taking evry thing. Camps full of chickens, butter & milk. Our mess had a chicken stew, cherries in great abundance. Nearly half the Reg'mt out foraging & can get almost any thing at your own price. This is a rich country, wheat very good & corn good, people very thickly setled & live in fine houses, nice gardens & seem to think more of their gardens & barns than any thing else, as they had the largest & finest Barns I ever saw. One farmer cultivates not over 10 acres. People all Dutch & some very poor. We are encamped in a grove & burnt all the fences around & wheat fields turned out. Our army living all-together on what we capture. Our advance infantry at or near "Harrisburg."

Drizling rain most the evening, we kept one sentinel on the watch all night in case of a surprise.

Thomas Ware

Horner's unit crosses the Monocacy River and marches through Buckeystown, Maryland, probably taking the most direct route, which would be along modern State Routes 28 and 85. Since Horner is not detailed in his description of

June 28

○ ○ ○   Ware's route   ● ● ●   Horner's route

the march, we can only assume which route he took; military necessity and spontaneous decisions on the part of officers in order to expedite the march may have taken Horner on slightly different roads than are described here. Generally, it is assumed they took the most direct route. Horner mentions where they camped, however, so we have a starting and ending point for each march.

They join up with the Fifth Army Corps, which is encamped near Frederick, Maryland, (probably just south of the town). For the current emergency, they will be attached to the Third Brigade, commanded by Col. Joseph W. Fisher, part of Brig. Gen. Samuel Crawford's Third Division, which is contained within the Fifth Corps, commanded by Maj. Gen. George Sykes.

Horner doesn't know it yet, nor does he consider it worthy enough anytime later to mention in his diary, but he has a new commanding general, George Gordon Meade. Major General Meade, formerly commander of the Fifth Corps, to which Horner's unit had just become attached, was awakened this day in the early morning hours and told that he now commands the entire Army of the Potomac. It cannot be an enviable position: In the midst of an active campaign, within a day or two's march of the enemy, who is threatening to capture his home state's capital, Meade goes from commanding one army corps to commanding eight times as many men, all needing to be fed, given enough ammunition and supplies for the upcoming battle, and, most important, told where to go—where to march to intercept the greatest threat to the nation's security in its history.

With Meade leaving the command of the Fifth Corps, that means that Maj. Gen. George Sykes will take over. Horner doesn't mention it; he probably doesn't even care. Like most soldiers in most wars throughout time, Horner has enough on his mind worrying about his sore feet, or whether his shoes will hold out, or what particular thing it is that keeps sticking him in the ribs while he walks, or whether he'll find a comfortable place to sleep when the march is over, or just how much longer this day's march will last.

Reading the Official Records—the officers' and government officials' correspondence during and action reports subsequent to the battle—it is amazing to find how confused, distracted, and even panic-stricken those in the highest positions are. Reading between the lines, you can discern petty jealousies, ramblings at meaningless inanities, prejudices, back-biting, and its corollary, defensiveness. You will finally realize that, as high up in the bureaucracy as they are, they really don't know what's going on any more than someone a hundred miles away would. The politicians eventually get the generals to act—often reluctantly, for legitimate military reasons—and the generals eventually get their troops to the right spot on the battlefield, and at the right time, if they are lucky. But always and forever, it has been the individual soldiers doing the fighting who decide the contest.

You can see it in both earlier and later wars, as when T. Grady Gallant describes marines fighting during the most geographically expansive campaign in military history, the Campaign in the Pacific in World War II.

> They moved through shellfire that could reduce steel plate and concrete and bolted iron to rubble. Their protection was the cloth against their bodies . . . and the rifle in their hands.
>
> Their protection was less than that of the Roman Legions, or the besiegers of a medieval castle. Yet they stormed, day after day, fortifications . . . and they destroyed them.
>
> It was by hand that the main line of . . . defenses was shattered. No aircraft did it. No artillery did it. No armored vehicles did it. It was done by the human hand. It was done by United States Marines on foot, clad in dungarees, moving across open badlands, crawling in gullies, approaching blockhouses in the face of murderous fire. It was done in this simple way. Caesar would have understood it.[98]

After the fight at Cold Harbor, and the assault through the cornfield at Antietam, and the frozen horror of Fredericksburg, Franklin Horner would have understood; after the vicious fight at

---

[98] Gallant, 170.

Garnett's farm, and Malvern Hill, and Sharpsburg, so would Thomas Ware.

Ware and the men of the 15th Georgia encamped the previous night about three miles north of Chambersburg. Obviously, General Lee's orders from the previous day reminding the men of their "forgetfulness" have not reached them yet. At least in some instances they pay for what they take. Unfortunately for Pennsylvania farmers, it is in Confederate currency, which may ease the conscience of a Southern soldier, but will be nonnegotiable for the farmer—unless, of course, the Rebels win the war.

For Ware it is a welcome day of rest after having marched seventy-two miles in the past four days.

June 29
○ ○ ○ *Ware's route*   ● ● ● *Horner's route*

Monday 29

had orders to march at day light but did not start till one P.M. we went in rear of the wagon train all day went past Frederick City we got to camp about 11 P.M. we marched about ten mile through a thriving wheat country had a little rain nothing from the front we are now nearly a day behind time so we have to make it up in marching boys all tired

Franklin Horner

June 29th. "Monday." 1863.

Cloudy & drizly day; Regimental Inspection very strict orders none permitted to leave Camps without a pass. A great many cherries brought to Camps. Q Masters are gathering all the horses around, beeves &c. Several the boys have seen fine horses tied out in the woods. I eat a great many cherries today. Cooking up 3 days rations of flour.

Our Reg'mt & 17 with others of the <u>Div</u> Sent to tear up & burn the R. R. We tore up all the ties & piled the Iron on it & burnt 4 miles the R. R. We burnt the bridge across the river at Scotland Station 5 miles of <u>Shippensburg</u>, the bridge was first burnt by our advance Cavalry & rebuilt next day after we fell back & we returned next day & bunt it again, it was a very costly one 50 feet high & 50 yards long. We did not burn the depot.

Returned back to Camps at dark & received orders to leave early in the morning.

Thomas Ware

The actual orders that animate Horner and the men of his unit are preserved in the *Official Records* and were issued by General Meade on June 28, 1863. Each army corps is given a general route to follow so that they will move during the day and arrive in the evening within supporting distance of one another, not hinder each other's march, and, most important, remain always between the enemy and Washington.

Fairly simple, the orders instruct that "The Fifth Corps will follow the Second Corps, moving at 8 A.M., camping at Union." Two paragraphs above, the Second Corps is ordered to move on June 28, at 4 A.M., ". . . by Johnsville, Liberty, and Union, to Frizellburg."

But, as happens all too often, the Fifth Corps, or at least the men of the 12th Pennsylvania Reserves, do not get under way until an hour after noon. Although the delay is probably no fault of Horner's unit, it is costly, and the men know who will eventually pay for it. They march long into the night, stumbling along dark summer roads, past Frederick, Maryland, and encamping near a town called Liberty.[99] Libertytown is located on modern State Route 26. Horner's march route cannot be determined quite as easily as Ware's, who mentions streams and railroads that he crosses most religiously, and which can be pinpointed today on modern maps. Piecing together other unit reports from the Fifth Corps helps, and we can surmise Horner's general route from the towns through which he passes.

Frederick, Maryland, once a small community of merchants and a supply center for the mountain people to the west and for generations of farmers who tilled the miles of fields spreading to the east, has become a town of condominiums for commuters to Washington. A fine attempt has been made at preserving and restoring some of the historical ambience of the downtown district, but the suburbs—especially south of Frederick, where Horner camped—have sprouted sprawling apartment complexes, although the simple stone farmhouse and bank barn can still, occasionally, be seen behind the condos.

The countryside through which Horner moves east of Frederick, however, is filled with long, rolling hills and small towns that have changed little since the passing of a great army. The roads are paved now and just a little wider than when the 12th Pennsylvania rapidly wore out shoe leather on them for a few frenetic

---

[99] *O.R.*, Vol. 27, Part 1, 595.

days in the summer of 1863. The hills abide in that section of Maryland and are just as taxing to the residents today, who must climb them to walk a block to their neighbors', as they have always been.

Ware's 15th Georgia, as well as the 17th Georgia and some other units, are sent northward along the railroad to destroy as much of it as they can. Railroad companies are historically protective of their rights-of-way, some of which were established in the 1830s and remain intact to this day. The railroad out of Chambersburg no doubt follows the same general line that it did during Ware's passage. Someone with a metal detector today could find an abundance of old spikes along the tracks, pulled up by the Georgians as they removed rails and tore up ties, and an abundance of unused minié balls, spilled as the warriors-turned-gandy dancers bent to move rails or removed their cartridge boxes and laid them down. A trained archaeologist could find evidence of burned piles of ties and other, more fragile, relics of the soldiers from the South who came this way before us.

The railroad bridge across the river at Scotland is made of stone and concrete now but does rise the fifty or so feet above the water as Ware saw the old bridge. Some of the houses in and around the tracks date back to before the Civil War, but it's difficult to pinpoint exactly which one, if it still stands, served as the depot.

The railroads in the Civil War, for the first time in history, became a major part of the war effort. They carried supplies, weapons, and even soldiers (as Ware noted when he passed through Piedmont Station on June 17), and because of their use by the armies, were as much legitimate targets for the infantry as merchant ships were for submarines in the World Wars.

While he mentions burning the railroads, which could only mean the wooden ties, Ware doesn't mention how they disposed of the iron rails. The standard procedure for William Tecumseh Sherman as he and his men marched through Ware's home state was to fire the ties, place the rails on top until they glowed, then have the men wrap the malleable rails around a nearby telegraph pole. The twisted and corkscrewed iron rails wrapped about the poles were dubbed "Sherman's neckties." Confederates may have

done the same thing in Pennsylvania, but the name would come at
a later time in the war.

Tuesday, June 30, 1863

took the line of march at seven A.M. were mustered for pay this morning went through Liberty, Union Bridge, Muttontown, and Uniontown and encamped close to town in a meddow about seven P.M. marched about twenty mile had colers flying and drums beating through all the towns to day rainde some had plent mud to wade all day boys all tired

Franklin Horner

June 30th. "Tuesday." 1863.

Cloudy & rainy day. Called in lines at 8, but did not leave 'till 9 A.M. We marched slowly (resting often) a country road leaving the town to our right road very crooked for 3 miles march We came in the "Harrisburg", "Chambersburg", Pen "Baltimore" M. D. pike, very good road to march. After 2 miles march we passed by "Hill's" Corps (or post). Encamped at the village of "Fayetteville". We left the pike at the village & marched a country road 2 miles & stopped to Camp at 1 P.M. We made fences fly.

Saw part the Irvin Artillery. I with several others went to a house near Camps & got a great many cherries I never saw the like before. We are encamped at the foot of the Mt. Several gone over it to look for horses, people mostly poor & very thickly setled. Very good Camps.

Capt Craft ordered to report at Atlanta Ga as Ass't Commissary. Sent a letter by him to have mailed to Pa. Wrote a letter to "J. B. F."

Drizly wet evening, have a splendid place to sleep, some dry straw. Had a splendid nights rest.

Thomas Ware

June 30

○ ○ ○ *Ware's route*   ● ● ● *Horner's route*

[Circular.]   Headquarters Army of the Potomac,
                                      June 29, 1863.
      The following is the order of march for to-
morrow:
      Twelfth Corps to Littlestown, passing the Third
Corps.
      Fifth Corps, Pipe Creek Crossing, on the road
between Littlestown and Westminster.[100]

So read the official orders sending Horner and his comrades
marching on June 30, 1863.

Twenty miles in one day. Twelve long hours of being on the
road. At a regular stride, a person should be able to walk a mile in
something between fifteen and twenty minutes. Without pack or
rifle or worn-out shoes or thousands of men and horses and wagons
clogging up the road in front, even under ideal conditions, twenty
miles is still about five or six straight hours of walking. Twenty
miles in twelve hours is 1.6 miles per hour average. Probably, because of all the halts and rest periods (if there were many), they
were striding along at 2 miles per hour or a little better. Any way
you break it down, and in spite of Horner's casual mention that
they "marched about twenty mile," this is one of the toughest
marches he's ever had to make.

The monthly salary for a private in the Union Army in 1863 was
$13. Horner, being a noncommissioned officer, drew more than
that.[101] "Mustering" for pay didn't necessarily mean the soldiers had
money in their pockets when they walked away. It merely meant
that, by showing up at the muster once a month and answering when
their names were called, they indicated they were present for duty in
order to get paid.[102] The money may not arrive for another several

---

[100] *O.R.,* Vol. 27, Part 3, 402.

[101] His military records show that Horner had been promoted from corporal to
first sergeant on August 3, 1861. According to Bates's *Martial Deeds of Pennsylvania*
(901) Horner was commissioned second lieutenant to date from July 8, 1862, but the
formal papers were not issued by Pennsylvania's governor Curtin until September 12,
1863. Nowhere else in his records is there mention of his promotion to officer's status,
nor was he even "mustered" as a lieutenant.

[102] Wiley, *The Life of Billy Yank,* 48-49.

months, but nobody wanted to miss the muster. Yet, while the thought of getting paid is nice, Horner and the rest of the 12th Pennsylvania Reserves have more important things to worry about.

Their officers know that the Confederate Army of Northern Virginia has been through York, Pennsylvania, and that in order for the Union Army to cover Washington and not allow the Confederates to swing around them to the east, they must march in this direction.

Libertytown, Union Bridge, and Uniontown all appear on modern maps of Maryland, so we can reconstruct Horner's march today. Coming from Frederick, he probably took modern State Route 26, which leads directly from the Frederick area to Libertytown. From there he took State Route 75, which leads through Johnsville (on the march route as ordered on June 28 for June 29) and to Union Bridge. "Muttontown" does not appear on either modern or historic maps, so the name may have been a colloquialism for another town or perhaps just a collection of farmhouses at a bend in the road where sheep were the predominant livestock. Horner's unit encamped for the night just outside of Uniontown.

It is difficult to imagine life in small-town America in the mid-nineteenth century and how the war was viewed by its civilian inhabitants. Most in the North would never see their towns touched by war, yet still they might suffer the sudden, strangulating shock of seeing the name of a loved one on the casualty list in the hometown paper. For many, that is as close as war would come.

To most civilians in Maryland and Pennsylvania, like those in Liberty and Union Bridge and Muttontown, the dust-coated, arm-swinging soldiers marching in step, rank by rank, with flags whipping above their heads, to bands playing stirring martial music would be their only image of war. A few may have seen the photographs taken by Mathew Brady and his assistants of nearby Sharpsburg after the battle there. Some may even have visited that field to return with nightmare stories of the torn and mutilated human forms, bloated, oily black and totally unearthly looking—stories that were hardly believed, even if they were completely comprehended.

One must wonder if Horner's comment about flags flying

and bands playing could have a ring of irony in it. He had been through the bloodiest day in American history just nine months before at Antietam.[103] He knows he's headed toward yet another confrontation with one of the finest and most deadly armies on the planet. Surely his reaction to the music and flags was different than that of the cheering residents of Muttontown.[104]

Modern U.S. Route 30, which was to be the modern highway to connect the East Coast to the West, follows much of the route of the old Chambersburg to Baltimore Pike, which Thomas Ware would eventually march. A good bit of it, however, bypasses some of the smaller towns like Fayetteville and Cashtown. There are a few small roads that lead off the main road and have streams near them, and Ware doesn't say exactly where he spent the night. But the road leading from Fayetteville to the northeast crosses another road, modern State Route 997, which cuts back into the Chambersburg and Baltimore Pike. Route 997 also leads into the mountains to the north. With an eye toward continuing to follow the lead elements of the Confederate Army northward using the mountains for a screen, or moving eastward to concentrate on that side of the South Mountains, or just making way for the rest of the army to pass, General Hood or General Benning probably chose to move off the main road to the north.[105] Ware mentions that they encamped at the foot of the mountains, which are north of the Chambersburg Pike.

Again, Ware's thoughts turn to home. Normally candid Ware,

---

[103] Horner Diary, September 17, 1862: "the battle commenced before day with all the vengence immagenable, lasted all day our Regiment was nearly anihilated." September 18: "we have about one hundred and fifty men left. our men are burrying the dead all day."

[104] Ibid., September 19, 1862: "marched about three miles went through the battle-field [Antietam] the dead are laying thick all over the battlefield and are becoming decomposed. . . . I am not well."

[105] *O.R.*, Vol. 27, Part 2, 307, Report of R. E. Lee, July 31, 1863: "Preparations were now made to advance upon Harrisburg; but, on the night of the 28th [of June], information was received from a scout that the Federal Army, having crossed the Potomac, was advancing northward, and that the head of the column had reached the South Mountain. As our communications with the Potomac were thus menaced, it was resolved to prevent his farther progress in that direction by concentrating our army on the east side of the mountains. Accordingly, Longstreet and Hill were directed to proceed from Chambersburg to Gettysburg, to which point General Ewell was also instructed to march from Carlisle."

who likes to name his friends in his diary entry, suddenly becomes shy when it comes to a certain individual. "<u>J. B. F.</u>" (or "<u>A. B. C.</u>" or "<u>D. E. F.</u>") is apparently someone very special who continues to remain etched in his thoughts and waits for him back in Lincolnton.

Ware and Horner are now about thirty-seven miles apart.

Wednesday, July 1, 1863

got into line at five A.M. and marched nearly all day went about fifteen mile are now in Penna York County and within five or six miles from the rebels expect to get into a fight to morrow heard some firing in our front this evening sent the baggage wagon all to the rear we expecting to march nearly all night weather pleasant all day

Franklin Horner

[Undated entry. Assumed to be July 1, 1863.]

A cloudy day. We have orders to prepare 3 days rations & be ready to march at a moments warning. Orders came to be ready to leave at 4 O'clock. Soon the drum beat & all in lines. Our Brigade (Benning's) in front. We passed through the village of Fayetteville. Here we took the Chambersburg & Baltimore turn pike. After marching all night we stoped at 4 O'clock and rested 3 hours.

Thomas Ware

It would be a mistake to use what we now know of the Battle of Gettysburg and in any way apply that to Horner's and Ware's experiences. But it would also be wrong to leave the reader in the dark about what is currently happening just a few miles away from them, of which both are aware only from the distant sounds and increased energy of the march. Hundreds of volumes have been written about the Battle of Gettysburg. They are suggested reading for later, but really have no relationship to what Franklin Horner and Thomas Ware know and see over the next few days.

The firing Horner mentions hearing in the distance is some of the last rounds being fired in the fighting north of Gettysburg on the evening of July 1, which had been going on since early that

July 1

○ ○ ○   Ware's route   ● ● ●   Horner's route

morning. Though both Horner and Ware mention nothing about the fighting earlier that day, occurrences at Gettysburg affect their march routes.

Union cavalry had encamped on the night of June 30 on the western and northern outskirts of Gettysburg, a small, rural southern Pennsylvania town with a population of about 2,400. The number of civilians in the town was probably greatly reduced by the first days of July, however, since most of the men had loaded their valuables on wagons and driven the livestock before them in an attempt to cross the Susquehanna River to the north before Confederates could confiscate the goods. For the most part, the Civil War was fought amongst armed men. Many of the women and children were left behind to watch over the possessions that could not be moved. In addition to the male farmers and merchants, most of the blacks who lived in Gettysburg fled, fearing capture by the Confederates and a life of slavery in the South.

Horner doesn't mention his location, but records confirm that by July 1, 1863, the Fifth Corps had marched to an area just west of Hanover, Pennsylvania, in York County and rested for the night near modern State Route 116.[106]

Looking at a map of the area, one realizes that Gettysburg is the point of convergence for about a dozen roads, and while neither Lee nor Meade specifically wanted to fight at Gettysburg, it makes sense that two huge armies marching through the area would brush against each other where the roads meet. And that's just what happened.

At about five A. M., Confederates near Cashtown, just a few miles east of Ware's unit, began marching toward Gettysburg.[107] They drove in the Federal cavalry videttes that had been posted several miles west of Gettysburg. By 8:30 or 9:00 A. M., they had advanced to engage the rest of the cavalry stretched out upon one of the several ridges that run generally north to south around the town. As soon as both sides determined that the enemy they had engaged was a sizable force, they sent for reinforcements, and the numerous units of both armies—including Thomas Ware's and

---

[106] *O.R.*, Vol. 27, Part 1, 595, 610, 621, 622, 633, 634, et al.
[107] Ibid., Part 2, 637.

Franklin Horner's—began moving toward Gettysburg as rapidly as they could.

While the 12th Pennsylvania Reserves are rushed toward the sound of the guns, the men of the 15th Georgia prepare food. Ware doesn't begin to march until 4:00 P. M. but has to march all night and into the dawn of July 2. They covered the ten miles from outside Fayetteville to an area west of Cashtown in twelve hours. It was a slow pace because the other units ahead of them are all jamming into the Chambersburg to Gettysburg Pike, and large numbers of wounded are beginning to be transported to the rear as Ware's unit approaches the battlefield.

Ware and Horner are about twelve miles apart.

Oddly, this day, July 1, the handwriting in Ware's diary changes.

Thursday 2

we marched last night till one A.M. marched about twenty
five mile in all yesterday started this morning at six O clock
and went about fifteen mile when we halted within sight of
the rebs now we expecting to march on the battlefield soon
evening we are on the battlefield and in line of battle the
boys are determined to drive the rebels out of the state the
battle is rageing fiercely now we will soon be in

Franklin Horner

You almost have to hold Franklin Horner's small, leather-
bound pocket diary in your hand and read it very slowly
aloud to understand the importance of his words. Punctu-
ating it correctly may help:

> We marched last night till one A.M. Marched
> about twenty-five miles in all yesterday. Started this
> morning at six o'clock and went about fifteen miles,
> when we halted within sight of the rebs.

The Official Records for the Union Army of the Potomac place
Crawford's Division containing Franklin's unit, from 1:00 A.M.
until daylight on July 2, at McSherrystown, just west of Hanover,
Pennsylvania.[108]

From McSherrystown they could have taken any one of the
several roads that crisscross the farmlands between McSherrystown
and Gettysburg. All General Crawford's report says is that "by
noon [the column] had arrived at the position occupied by the
First and Second Divisions of the corps, near the Gettysburg and
Hanover turnpike."[109]

---

[108] *O.R.*, Vol. 27, Part 1, 652.
[109] Ibid., 653. This position is corroborated by the report of Brig. Gen. Romeyn
Ayres, commanding the Second Division, ibid., 634.

GETTYSBURG

July 2
○ ○ ○ *Ware's route* ● ● ● *Horner's route*

Horner's march probably took him along the Hanover to Gettysburg Road (modern State Route 116). From there all three divisions of Sykes's Fifth Corps moved to the south, eventually ending up near the Taneytown Road, in the rear of the main Union battleline:

> ... now we expecting to march on the battlefield soon ....

General Crawford's report, written just a week after the battle, is very detailed as to the movements of his troops and, thanks to hindsight and reflection from the position of an officer, adds a great deal to Horner's terse entries:

> At 2 o'clock an order reached me to form my command at once, and proceed toward the left flank of our line, when my position would be indicated by a staff officer. The First Division of the corps, which I

West face of Little Round Top. "We are on the battlefield and in line of battle."

had been directed to follow, had taken a different road from that indicated to me. Under the guidance, however, of Captain Moore, an aide of the general commanding the army, who had come from the field for fresh troops, I pushed rapidly forward, and arrived in a short time upon the field, and reported to Major General Sykes. I received orders at once to mass my troops upon the right of a road running through our line, near our left flank, and which, descending a rocky slope, crossed a low marshy ground in front to a wheat-field lying between two thick belts of woods beyond.

The position occupied by our troops on the left was naturally a strong one. A rocky ridge, wooded at the top, extended along the left of our position, ending in a high hill, called the Round Top, whose sides, covered with timber, terminated abruptly in the plain below, while the entire ridge sloped toward a small stream that traversed the marshy ground in front.[110]

From Crawford's vivid and accurate description of the terrain, we can ascertain that Horner and the men of the 12th Pennsylvania are beginning to be positioned just to the north of the Millerstown Road, or, as it has been called since the battle, the Wheatfield Road. From their position, the men can see the slopes of Little Round Top, Round Top, and the valley between those hills and Houck's Ridge and Devil's Den. Before the division finishes getting into position, however, Crawford receives another order:

The movement indicated had not been completed when I received a subsequent order to cross the road to the slope of the rocky ridge opposite the woods, and to cover the troops then engaged in front, should it become necessary for them to fall back.[111]

---

[110] *O.R.*, Vol. 27, Part 1, 653.
[111] Ibid.

Returning to Horner's diary, with punctuation added:

> Evening. We are on the battle field and in line of
> battle. The boys are determined to drive the rebels
> out of the state. The battle is raging fiercely now. We
> will soon be in.

Somewhere along the boulder-strewn west slope of Little
Round Top, Franklin Horner, unsure whether in ten minutes he
would be alive or dead, stands in line with the rest of the men of
the 12th Pennsylvania, pulls out his tiny pocket diary, and scrawls
those words. Coming from about two hundred yards in front of
him just on the other side of a short ridge that ends in a jumble of
boulders, Horner can hear the fighting for that ridge and the pile
of rocks known to the local people as Devil's Den. Just beyond
Devil's Den is a three-sided, sloping farm field, which is being
crossed by the first of three charges the Confederates were to make
in an attempt to dislodge the Union troops from Devil's Den.
Hearing the rattling musketry and seeing the white smoke boil
from behind the rocks like some hideous cauldron, Horner must
be certain he was headed into the inferno.

Suddenly General Crawford gets an order to detach a brigade
from his division and send it to the left of General Barnes's Division, holding the ridge behind them.

> I received instructions to detach one brigade of
> my command to go to the left of Barnes' division, on
> the crest of the ridge. The Third Brigade, under Col.
> J. W. Fisher, was detailed, and moved at once. The
> firing in our front was heavy and incessant. The
> enemy, concentrating his forces opposite the left of
> our line, was throwing them in heavy masses upon
> our troops, and was steadily advancing.[112]

Horner's unit, as part of Fisher's brigade, moves off to the left
into what was appearing to be an extension of the vicious fighting
Horner had been witnessing.

---

[112] *O.R.*, Vol. 27, Part 1, 653.

In the meantime, Thomas Ware, who had started his march at 7:00 A.M., finally arrives at Gettysburg after following the Chambersburg Road from Cashtown (modern Route 30).

According to the official report of Lt. Col. William S. Shepherd, 2nd Georgia Regiment of Benning's brigade, the brigade arrived about noon July 2 upon the fields west of Gettysburg where the fighting of the previous day had occurred.[113] That would place Ware between where Willoughby Run crosses the Chambersburg to Gettysburg Pike and the west slope of Seminary Ridge where they rest.

July 2nd. "Thursday." 1863.

We received orders to be ready to march at 7 O'clock. Soon we were in marching order and left for the Scene of action. Passing through Cashtown and marching one hour we came in sight of Gettysburg. Here we rested in an old field until 2 O'clock, at which time we left to Attack the Enemy. After passing through a very heavy shelling for 20 minutes we rested and then formed a line of battle....

Ware Diary

This part of the July 2 account in Ware's diary corresponds to both Brigadier General Benning's brigade report and the report of Ware's regimental commander, Col. D. M. Du Bose. According to Benning:

About 2 or 3 P.M. on July 2, ultimo, I was informed by Major-General Hood that his division, as the right of Lieutenant General Longstreet's Corps, was about to attack the left of the enemy's line, and that in the attack my brigade would follow Law's brigade at the distance of about 400 yards. In order to get to the place assigned me, in the rear of General Law, it was necessary to move the brigade 500 or 600

---

[113] *O.R.*, Vol. 27, Part 2, 420, 424.

> yards farther to the right. Having done this, I ad-
> vanced in line of battle. A wood intervened between
> us and the enemy, which, though it did not prevent
> their shells from reaching us and producing some
> casualties, yet completely hid them from view.[114]

Du Bose also mentions that they moved "under a heavy shelling" from the enemy.[115]

Oddly, what Benning, Du Bose, and the July 2 entry in Ware's diary all fail to mention is that they were part of a strange march and countermarch to reach their final position of assault. Though much has been made of "Longstreet's Flank March," implying that it was a delaying tactic by Lee's most trusted subordinate and may have cost the battle, most of the implications are unfounded. Although the march took up two to three hours' time, relative to what took place after the men were in position, it warranted only the comment that it was a "circuitous" march by just two of the four regimental commanders in Benning's brigade.[116]

Ware and the 15th Georgia, as part of Benning's brigade, marched from their original position on the first day's battlefield back out the Chambersburg Road, south along a back road along Marsh Creek west of Gettysburg, then reversed their direction, cutting across fields until they reached Willoughby Run, closer to Gettysburg. This "circuitous" route was necessitated by the fear among the Confederate leaders of the march that Union signal-men on Little Round Top had discovered them. The march appar-ently took up the time between the rest "in an old field until 2 O'clock P.M." and when they were in position to begin their attack.

They generally followed Willoughby Run south about three miles to a staging area near the Emmitsburg Road (modern State Route 15) in preparation for a sweep northward against the south-ern end of the Union line. However, as they march through the woods following other troops according to orders,[117] they find

---

[114] *O.R.*, Vol. 27, Part 2, 414.

[115] Ibid., 421.

[116] Ibid., 420 (Lt. Col. William S. Shepherd's report of the 2nd Georgia Infantry); 425 (Col. Wesley C. Hodges's report of the 17th Georgia Infantry).

[117] Actually, General Benning followed the wrong troops into the battle, mistak-ing Robertson's brigade for Law's.

themselves supporting an attack by Robertson's brigade against a line of artillery and infantry posted behind a stone wall at the top of a rock-cluttered slope.

The battlefield upon which Thomas Ware and the men of the 15th Georgia struggled is remarkably compact: Virtually all of the area over which they attacked can be seen with a sweep of the eye. The 15th Georgia's attack had the unit straddling a stone wall as it moved up the hill through woods on its left and through an oddly shaped triangular field owned by a local farmer, G. W. Weikert.[118] With the exception of some exploratory quarrying holes dug after the war, the area has been cleared by the National Park Service and restored to its 1863 appearance. Today we can stand and wander at leisure the field where cows graze; when Thomas Ware saw it, however, there was the white haze of black-powder smoke hanging in the windless evening and the red haze of fear and nervous anticipation that fighting men call the "fog of battle" blacking out much of the warriors' perceptions.

To the soldier, there has been across the millennia, despite advancing technologies and tactics, but one kind of war, forever and ever. And that is the war whose parameters are exactly the distance from where a man stands to where the smoke and dust and fear blot out the extent of his experiences. It has been the length of an assagai spear, or the space between the waist-gun windows of a B-17, or the few yards' distance from the flash guard of an M-16 to where the claustrophobic jungle conceals the enemy. But it has been the same forever, this small, singular kind of war, and it lasts only minutes or maybe—rarely—an hour, and then it is over, immutable, yet changing everything.

Now things begin to happen quickly. From Colonel Du Bose:

> I immediately ordered a forward movement, and soon gained the point where our advance troops were fighting behind a stone fence, a little above the foot of a high, wooded, rocky hill. At this point my regiment commenced the engagement

---

[118] Harrison, 57–58.

with the enemy, who occupied the hill. At this point,
the nature of the ground was such that I could not
see the other portion of the brigade.[119]

Today from that position, with the woods thick in summer
foliage and the way the terrain drops off, it is easy to see that Du
Bose and the men of the 15th Georgia, even though they were on
the extreme left end of the brigade line, could not see the rest of the
brigade.

From Ware's diary:

> We charged the enemy, driving them from their
> position. . . .

Du Bose's report:

> I immediately ordered my regiment to jump the
> stone fence, and charge that portion of the hill in
> my front, which order they obeyed willingly and
> promptly, driving the enemy from my part of the
> hill. . . . In this charge, a portion of one of the Texas
> regiments (the First Texas) joined me, and behaved
> well.[120]

Actually, the First Texas had been repulsed earlier in a counterattack by the 124th New York, had broken and retreated disorganized into the 15th Georgia. The officers tried for several minutes to disentangle the units but gave up, and the units fought
together for the rest of the battle.[121]

Du Bose reported that he had taken his regiment between a
quarter and a half mile beyond the top of the ridge when he saw a
large force of Union troops moving so as to cut him off from his
support. He ordered the regiment to fall back to its original position at the stone fence.[122]

---

[119] *O.R.,* Vol. 27, Part 2, 421.
[120] Ibid., 422.
[121] Harrison, 49.
[122] *O.R.,* Vol. 27, Part 2, 422.

Looking to their left, Ware and the men of the 15th see a Confederate regiment preparing to charge back up the hill. Now, with support nearby, Colonel Du Bose orders his men to charge again, "which they did well, driving the enemy from their position."[123]

After the second charge, the infantry on the 15th Georgia's left retire and another large column of the enemy appear, driving in the Georgians' skirmishers on the left flank. Du Bose, the 15th Georgia, and Ware once again are forced to fall back to the stone wall.

Du Bose then receives a message from the commander of the troops to his left saying that he was going to charge the enemy one more time, "which proposition I agreed to at once, and immediately ordered my regiment forward, and again did they obey the order with alacrity and courage, driving the enemy this time entirely out of the woods in my front."[124]

This third charge is only temporarily successful, but, in one small sense, exceedingly costly. From Thomas Ware's diary:

> Here at the foot of the mountain the engagement became general & fierce & lasted until 8 O'clock at night. And in the third & last charge the fatal blow was struck.
>
> My Brother: You have offered your life as a sacrifise upon your country's Altar.
>
> Today concludes the term of life of my Brother. He now sleeps upon the battle field of Gettysburg with

> There Brothers, Fathers, small & great,
> Partake the same repose
> There in peace the ashes mix
> Of those who once were foes

> *Robert Ware*

Now we can understand why the handwriting in Thomas Ware's precious diary changed so abruptly July 1. It was no longer Thomas who had been writing in his diary after June 30; it was his

---

[123] *O.R.,* Vol. 27, Part 2, 422.
[124] Ibid.

younger brother Robert, who, heartbroken, took the diary from Thomas's haversack and gently continued the daily entries, as if trying to keep his brother alive for a few more days. Finally he brought himself to record his older brother's death in battle.[125]

By the time the 15th Georgia made the third charge up Weikert's Triangular Field, Smith's Battery of Union Artillery, which had been firing from the top of the Triangular Field, had been silenced. The guns remaining on the horizon, however, were a threatening reminder that they could be brought to life again at any moment.

The Georgians and Texans were being fired at by the remnants of the 124th New York—the same unit that had driven the Texans into the Georgians' line in the first place. As well, during the last charge, the 99th Pennsylvania was firing into the 15th and the 20th Georgia just to its right. Finally, Lt. Charles Hazlett's Battery D, 5th U.S. Artillery, on Little Round Top, was lobbing into the Triangular Field shells that caromed off the rocks and earth or exploded overhead. Ware could have been killed by a minié ball from the New Yorkers or the Pennsylvanians; he could have been torn apart by ten pounds of exploding iron from Hazlett's Battery. In combat, it is not unusual for men to be wounded or killed by parts of other soldiers—a fragment of skull, a piece of femur, a tooth—driven at lethal speed by a bullet or shell. We will never know how he was killed. But thankfully, Ware's younger brother was there to identify the body. Perhaps, if he were unlucky enough to be looking in the right direction, Robert saw his own brother killed.

A review of Union general Crawford's account reveals that the division was witness to the fighting that is described in Ware's diary:

> I received instructions to detach one brigade of my command, to go to the left of Barnes division, on the crest of the ridge. The Third Brigade, under Col. J. W. Fisher, was detailed, and moved at once. The firing in front was heavy and incessant.[126]

---

[125] Thomas Ware wrote his last diary entry on June 30, 1863, two days before his death. Robert continued the diary as if he were Thomas until his own capture as a prisoner of war on July 3.

[126] *O.R.*, Vol. 27, Part 1, 653.

And again from Horner's diary:

The battle is rageing fiercely now. . . .

This was the fighting in which Thomas Ware was killed.

Many of our brother soldiers whose life was made a sac-
rifise upon our country's altar. There the weeping willow
gently waves over his grave. And there we prayed that
God would guard and protect that little mound.

Robert Ware

It is so easy to forget, when casualties number in the
thousands, that there are faces, and bodies, and personalities that
die. It is easy, sitting in one's study reading, to gloss over the terrible

*The Triangular Field. "And in the third & last charge the fatal blow was
struck."*

waste and loss to others: Thomas Ware's parents, who would never forget their firstborn; Robert, who would live with the memories of seeing his beloved older brother, for whom he had transferred into the regiment, killed in battle and of burying him on the field; and "<u>A. B. C.</u>," who would wait no more for Thomas's letters or his return home.

Many of the dead from the fighting in the area of Devil's Den and Weikert's Triangular Field were taken to the rear and buried near the Slyder, Rose and Bushman farms and along the banks of Plum Run, where, indeed, in the soft, damp earth weeping willows grow.[127]

It would be interesting to know how long Robert would have continued to keep his brother's diary going if he himself hadn't been captured in the fighting on the very next day.

---

[127] Richter, 119. In a telephone interview on March 3, 1992, Mr. Richter confirmed that several Confederates were buried at the Bushman Farm and that, according to Dr. J. W. C. O'Neal, a prominent Gettysburg resident who attempted to list all the Confederates still buried on the battlefield in 1866, Thomas Ware, 15th Georgia Infantry, was indeed one of those.

Friday, July 3, 1863

we charged sugar loaf mountain last night and took posession without firing a shot part of our Regiment got lost and
got out side of our Pickets but we got back again and now
are on the hill and have rifle pits we stayed on the hill all
day without fighting any the battle last all day the heaviest
artilery fight commenced at two P. M. and lasted for two
hours the rebs got the worst of the fight they a great many
prisoners.

Franklin Horner

H orner had obviously been too busy on the evening of July 2
to record the day's action in his diary.

The part of Crawford's Division that remained when Horner's
unit was detached saw their own Union troops disorganized and
retreating from the Confederate attacks up the slopes of Weikert's
Triangular Field and through Devil's Den. They were being followed closely by large numbers of the enemy. Crawford aligned
his remaining regiments in two lines and ordered an advance.

The command advanced gallantly with loud
cheers. Two well-directed volleys were delivered
upon the advancing masses of the enemy, when the
whole column charged at a run down the slope, driving the enemy back across the space beyond and
across the stone wall, for the possession of which
there was a short but determined struggle. The
enemy retired to the wheat-field and the woods.[128]

After his Union troops seemed to have driven the Confederates back, Crawford then rode over to the left to check on Fisher's

---

[128] *O.R.*, Vol. 27, Part 2, 653.

Brigade. From the summit of the smaller hill to the north of Round Top (which has been called Little Round Top since the battle), he could see and feel the annoying and dangerous effects of Confederate skirmishers on the larger hill firing down into the Union troops. Crawford ordered Horner's regiment along with the 5th Pennsylvania Reserves and the 20th Maine—a regiment from Barnes's Division that had just been in a fight for its very life—up the slope of Round Top (also referred to in some accounts as Sugar Loaf) to drive off the skirmishers.

Apparently, in the darkening woods of Round Top, Horner and some of the skirmishers got lost between the lines.

Horner then goes on to describe the events of July 3. From his point of view—that of the common soldier, most likely shared by thousands of other soldiers at Gettysburg—he gives his version of what has come to be known as one of the greatest infantry assaults of all time: Pickett's Charge. All Horner knows of it on July 3 is that there was a tremendous, two-hour cannonade starting, by his watch, at 2:00 P.M. (Most sources place the artillery bombardment's beginning at about 1:00.) By 3:00 (4:00 by Horner's watch), the assault of about 12,000 Confederates from Pickett's and parts of two other divisions had begun their march across the open fields between the two lines, about a mile and a half from where Horner stood.

Horner and his comrades may have been victims of the same rumor that was running along behind the right of the Union lines, spread by some overzealous orderly and heard by Union cavalry commander Judson Kilpatrick: "We turned the charge; nine acres of prisoners!"[129] The courier's misinformed zealousness in turn may have been what led General Kilpatrick to order young Brig. Gen. Elon J. Farnsworth on an ill-advised cavalry charge through woods, over fences, and around boulders, killing the young general and a number of his men.

By 5:00 P.M. on July 3, General Crawford had returned to the regiments he had left to check on Fisher's Brigade and received an order from his commander, General Sykes, to drive the enemy from their front. In his report he mistakes Benning's men for

[129] Parsons, 393.

Anderson's—both brigades of Georgians—and confuses several other details, such as the number of prisoners taken and the size of the force he fought.[130]

In reality, Crawford's men charged and struck one lone regiment left stranded by a mix-up in orders—the 15th Georgia—capturing the regimental flag under which Thomas Ware had marched, fought, and died, and several dozen prisoners, among whom was Robert Andrews Ware.

In his possession was the diary of his older brother.

---

[130] Coddington, 534.

Saturday 4

> we are still in the same place on the hill some skirmishing nearly all day no cannonading I think the rebels are leaving as fast as they can had a very heavy rain this evening moved our Regiment some to the right where we will stay the night our men are burrying the dead as fast as they can all quiet this evening
>
> *Franklin Horner*

Though Horner doesn't mention it, it had begun to rain in the morning and continued most of the day, getting fairly heavy at several times toward evening.

Contrary to what he observes and records, the Confederate Army was not in full retreat but merely pulling back some segments of its lines, consolidating, straightening, and digging rifle

Big Round Top (right). "We are still in the same place on the hill."

pits to ward off a Union counterattack that Lee had been expecting since the failure of Pickett's Charge. It never came.

There are no more entries in Ware's diary. Though Robert was as articulate as Thomas and seemed, at first, to wish to continue the entries, perhaps the reality of his brother's death had finally sunk in. Probably he was harried by his own capture and subsequent movement to the rear of the Union lines; no doubt he was despondent over the sudden death of Thomas and his own removal from friends in the 15th Georgia, and even frightened by what his captors might have in store for him. For whatever reason, the diary of Thomas Lewis Ware, and our road to his most intimate thoughts and feelings, has come to an end.

did not sleep well last night rained to much all quiet this morning went over the battlefield to day the sight of battle-field when the dead are lying there for two days in the hot sun is enough to make any man sick of war. we started to march at 7 P.M. and marched til 11 P.M. a distance of 7 mile when we encamped for the night in [illegible] field we had plenty of mud to wade all the way the rebels have left and we are after them as fast as we can go.

Franklin Horner

Stretching the imagination to its limits, one cannot begin to picture what the fields and woods around Gettysburg must have been like in the days after the battle.

Numbers help, but they are so overwhelming as to be almost meaningless, since they go beyond any experience most people have ever had.

Currently, Gettysburg National Military Park uses the figure of 44,000 casualties—that's killed, wounded, and missing—on both sides after three days of slaughter. Official figures at one time were as high as 51,000 casualties. Forty-four thousand. Fifty-one thousand. They are merely words unless one remembers that most modern football stadiums seat somewhere in the vicinity of 50,000. It's a fairly simple thing, then, the next time we're watching a game, to picture all or most of the people in the crowd killed, wounded, or missing, plopped down, helpless, in the tiny town of Gettysburg—population, 2,400—filling the fields, barns, churches, outbuildings, and private homes to overflowing.

Everywhere Horner looked there were bodies, some motion-less in death, but many still writhing, arms waving, giving the fields a singular crawling effect as far as could be seen.

There are photographs available of the dead after several

days, showing oily, blackened bodies swollen by internal gases to the point of bursting waistcoats and pants buttons, eyes bulging out, tongues bloated and sticking from dirty mouths as if hideously mocking those who live and must deal with them somehow. Most of the seriously wounded evacuated their bowels and bladders involuntarily; those who were wounded and could not move for two or three days did it on purpose, without any other choice; many of the dead had their bodies emptied of waste materials when they were eviscerated by a shell.

Even for those not wounded there wasn't time to observe all the rules of camp cleanliness. During the first four or five days in July, more than 170,000 men—many with acute diarrhea from lousy food or just plain fear—used Gettysburg as one vast outdoor toilet. Close to 90,000 horses—each producing about ten pounds of manure a day—were also on the field. Simple calculations for the horses alone yield 900,000 pounds of manure per day, or 2,700,000 for three days—3,600,000 if you include July 4. Add to that the daily excretions of the men. This is not meant to make light of what happened at Gettysburg, but to put it into perspective with our clean, virtually odorless streets. Even without the stench of the dead bodies and amputated limbs, Gettysburg would have been an abomination to the nostrils.

Of the 90,000 horses that were at Gettysburg, 5,000 were killed. After they were left in the hot sun for several days, someone decided that burning them would be the best thing, since a horse takes too much time and effort to bury; so 4,500,000 pounds of rotting horsemeat, bones, and sweat-soaked horsehair were then collected and burned.

And there, omnipresent, were the dead: tucked in the crevices of Devil's Den, tossed carelessly along the slopes of the Round Tops, littering the fields of Pickett's Charge, and, forgotten behind the lines on the first day's battlefield, those who crawled into the shelter of the railroad cut and there died. Some were still boys, some older men, illiterate private soldiers and highly educated officers, who died quickly or suffered in seemingly endless and brutish agony until they too died alone in numberless fence corners and cellars.

There were the sons and husbands and fathers and brothers.

If we accept John Busey's and David Martin's latest figures, the Union and Confederate armies at Gettysburg left about 7,700 dead men on the battlefield.[131] Actually, there were probably between 1,000 and 2,000 more than that, because tucked somewhere in the combined figures of 10,800 missing are not only those captured and sent to the prison pens, but also those who were unidentifiable even to men who had lived with them daily because they had been so completely liquefied by a shell or an exploding caisson, shrapnel, or canister.

So if we use the figures of 8,000 to 9,000, that means that somewhere between 1,200,000 and 1,350,000 pounds of putrifying human flesh were left lying around for several days in July. Perhaps the truly courageous ones were those who stayed to clean up.

Let's not forget those wounded in the extremities. A wound in the arm or leg nearly always drew the surgeon's knife and saw, and the limb that had served so well in walking and marching, catching in the games of "ball" the soldiers played, or writing letters home was suddenly lopped off by a surgeon grown callous by the sheer numbers of legs and arms and hands and feet he's amputated in the last hour. Those limbs, once so dear to the owners, were tossed ignominiously into piles in corners or out nearby windows, then wheelbarrowed out to be dumped in the fields, where they were eventually buried.

The flies came first, almost as soon as the wounds were opened or the dead were still. Feasting on the carrion, they grew so fat they fell from flight into the live soldiers' suppers, to be scooped out and tossed away before further consumption. They laid their eggs in the dead men's mouths and ears and eyes and nostrils, and maggots by the billions crawled until they too became flies and continued the cycle. Then came the vultures. And, finally, the burial parties, "burrying the dead as fast as they can."

But no one at home knew about that. No one at home ever knows about that. One wonders if in the Victorian Era humans still had to go through the same psychological stages after the sudden death of a loved one: unbelief; anger; denial; depression; and, finally, acceptance. Or was their stricter society, which mandated

---

[131] Busey and Martin.

that a woman put on mourning for an entire year for her loved one, an easier one in which to cope with death? One thinks not.

Lincoln had a terrible time accepting death, allegedly visiting the grave of a sweetheart in the pouring rain and spending hours in the crypt of his beloved son Willie. Stanton, his steely secretary of war, allegedly dug up the body of his child to continue his mourning. Mary Todd Lincoln raved after the death of her husband. No, it couldn't have been any easier.

Where were those who shouted loudest that they were on the holy crusade to save the Union or to rescue their Southern Rights? Where were those who, unlike Horner and Ware, saw this war as black and white with no grays? They were the ones who stayed at home, fighting for States' Rights from their offices, freeing the slaves from their pulpits, saving the Union from their congressional seats and saving their own skins as well.

But at Gettysburg, on July 5, 1863, there were only the quick and the dead.

Postbellum

Franklin Horner remained in the Union Army for another ten months, until he was honorably discharged at Harrisburg, Pennsylvania, on June 11, 1864.

He returned to Taylor Township, Cambria County, eventually becoming employed at a local sawmill. In August 1866 he lost the first two fingers of his right hand to a circular saw.[132]

On July 1, 1869, near Johnstown, Pennsylvania, he was married by the Reverend M. J. Montgomery to a woman from his old neighborhood, Sarah Alice Killin, whom he called Sallie. It was the first marriage for both.[133] During the next eleven years they had four children: Samuel J., born September 29, 1870; Daniel K., born January 1, 1873; William D., born May 7, 1875; and Daisy M., born June 22, 1881.

Sometime around 1894, Franklin and Sallie (and probably Daisy, who would still have been a child) moved from the city of Pittsburgh, where they had been living, into a two-story frame house on the corner of Swissvale and Sherman Streets in Wilkinsburg, Allegheny County, Pennsylvania, a small town near Pittsburgh.

By August 1898, Horner, now in his early sixties, first applied for a government pension by reason of "infirmity of old age and the loss of two first fingers on right hand." There are no records in the file saying whether he received the pension, but on October 13,

---

[132] National Archives, Department of the Interior, Bureau of Pensions, Franklin Horner Files: Declaration for Invalid Pension, dated August 20, 1898; affidavits on file of J. S. Snyder, who knew Horner for forty years, and D. W. Angus, for whom Horner was sawing at the time of the accident. Angus states: "he [Angus] was not just present at the time but within call and he came to the mill and saw the pieces on the saw yet. That is pieces of his fingers."

[133] Ibid., General Affidavit of Louisa [Horner] Gamble, August 8, 1904.

1900, he reapplied, requesting that he be allowed to appear before the Pension Office's board of examiners. (In this second application he appoints himself as his own attorney, apparently disappointed with the attorney in Washington to whom he had paid a $10 fee two years before to prosecute his first claim.)

On July 30, 1904, Franklin Horner, after an illness of one week, died of pneumonia. On or around August 1, he was buried in Woodlawn Cemetery, Wilkinsburg.

On August 4, 1904, sixty-five-year-old Sallie began to apply for her share of her late husband's pension, which the government held up beginning in July 1904 after his death. The pension at that time amounted to $6 per month. Numerous affidavits appear in the file, including testimony from her son Samuel, estimating their house's worth at about $4,200, the value of the 80-by-122-foot lot on the corner of Swissvale and Sherman Streets, and approximately what his mother's rent, expenses, and net worth would be. Horner still owed about $3,200 on the property, having mortgaged the property to pay off debts and improve the place.

The last pension payment to Sallie was paid on October 4, 1917. It amounted to $20. On December 13, 1917, Sallie Horner died in Wilkinsburg, Pennsylvania, and was buried next to her husband in Woodlawn Cemetery.

On September 27, 1910, Pennsylvania governor Edwin S. Stuart dedicated the Pennsylvania Monument, the largest one on the battlefield of Gettysburg. In addition to the bronze statues of President Abraham Lincoln and Andrew Curtin, governor of Pennsylvania during the Civil War, there are inscribed on bronze regimental plaques the names of more than 34,000 Pennsylvanians who fought in the Battle of Gettysburg.[134] Located on the plaque for the 12th Pennsylvania Reserves (41st Regiment of Infantry) is the name of Sgt. Franklin Horner.

In the crowd of Pennsylvania veterans who watched the unveiling of the monument was a Mr. T. H. Ryan of Kane, Kean County, Pennsylvania.

Robert Ware, after his capture, had been transported to the Union prison at Point Lookout, Maryland, at the mouth of the

---

[134] Tilberg.

Potomac River, where he spent the next nineteen months, until paroled on February 18, 1865, and furloughed home February 21.

For a number of years, Robert assumed that Thomas remained buried at Gettysburg. According to an article in the Lincolnton, Georgia, newspaper dated November 24, 1910, a Mr. T. H. Ryan of Kane, Pennsylvania, had written sometime before to Capt. "Tip" Harrison of Atlanta, inquiring about members of the 15th Georgia who were captured at the Battle of Gettysburg. Unable to provide very much information himself, Harrison had the letter published in several daily newspapers in Georgia, hoping to stir the interest of any members of the 15th who had been captured at Gettysburg.

The article was read by Robert Andrews Ware, who immediately wrote a letter to Ryan. Unfortunately, the letter came too late for Ryan's purposes. He had wanted to meet with any members of the 15th whom he might have fought against and go over the old battle sites once more. Robert's letter arrived at Ryan's residence in Kane while Ryan was visiting Gettysburg and attending the unveiling of the grand monument, which was to hold his name along with all the other Pennsylvanians who had fought at Gettysburg.

Apparently, Robert believed that Ryan had been the Union soldier who had captured him on July 3, 1863. He described the man to Ryan, and Ryan, in a letter dated October 17, 1910, two weeks after his visit to Gettysburg, said that yes, it was an accurate description of him as he had appeared during the war, but he could not remember the circumstances of Robert Ware's capture. He did remember meeting Col. Stephen Z. Harnesberger (also spelled Hearnsberger) of the 15th Georgia, who had also been captured on July 3.

Along with the October 17 letter, Ryan sent Robert a "Bucktail"—a deer tail that the men of his regiment wore in their caps as an identifying symbol—and a Grand Army of the Republic badge. Robert responded by forwarding his badge from the last Georgia State Reunion of Confederate Veterans and a few other relics from his home state.[135] In that second letter, which has never been found, Robert apparently asked T. H. Ryan to do him a favor and inquire at Gettysburg about the burial site of his brother and fellow soldier, Thomas.

---

[135] Kenneth Norman, personal files.

In the family archives of the Ware family, there is a letter from Calvin Hamilton, superintendent of the U.S. National Cemetery at Gettysburg, to Mr. T. H. Ryan. (Coincidentally, the letter is dated November 19, 1910—the 47th anniversary of Lincoln's Gettysburg Address dedicating the National Cemetery.) It states the following:

> In reply to your inquiry for a record of the grave Thos. L. Ware, Co G. 15th Georgia Regt. I regret to say that there is no record at this cemetery of any of the Confederate dead left on this field. All of their dead that could be found were taken up two or three years after the war by Confederate Associations and taken south, most of them to Hollywood Cemy., Richmond. Possibly by writing to the Officer in charge of Hollywood Cemetery Richmond, Va. you could learn whether the remains of Ware were identified and his grave marked.

If either Ryan or Robert inquired at Hollywood Cemetery in Richmond, they would have been disappointed. Thomas Ware was not listed as being buried in Hollywood. Robert must have thought for the rest of his life that his brother Thomas was buried in either Hollywood in one of the huge sections for unknown soldiers or beneath the "little mound" under the weeping willow tree near the Bushman Farm at Gettysburg.

While doing research for this book, I discovered in the Gettysburg National Military Park Archives a typescript of an article by William C. Storrick that appeared under the title "Battlefield Notes—Story of Col. Joseph Wasden" in the July 24, 1926, issue of the *Gettysburg Compiler*.

Wasden was colonel of the 22nd Georgia Regiment. The story revolves around the burial of Wasden near the Codori Barn at Gettysburg. In the article, Storrick quotes a letter from Dr. R. B. Weaver, in charge of the removal of the Confederate dead from the battlefield, to Dr. J. W. C. O'Neal, a prominent physician in Gettysburg during the mid-nineteenth century.

During the summer of 1872, per contract with

the Savannah Memorial Association, I exhumed the remains of Col. Wasden, and those one hundred Georgians who were buried on the Battlefield of Gettysburg, and shipped the same to the S. M. Ass'n, by whom they were reinterred in the Cemetery at Savannah, Ga. . . . I exhumed the remains of Col. W. and packed them in a large box, No. 5, in company with those of eight other Georgians, whose names were known as their graves had been marked. The remains were not packed separately in small boxes, but collectively in large boxes by direction of the Savannah Memorial Association to meet the limited capacity of the Soldiers Lot in the Cemetery.

In the file marked "Savannah, Georgia, Ladies Memorial Association" are the minutes for several of its meetings. The minutes for the April 20, 1872, meeting state that "During the year 101 bodies of Georgia soldiers were brought from Gettysburg & interred in 'Laurel Grove Cemetary.' Expended for the same $410."

Was Thomas Ware exhumed with that group of Georgians in the summer of 1872 and taken to Savannah? A phone call to the Georgia Historical Society in Savannah on February 10, 1987, and a search by historian Tracy Bearden revealed that a "J. Ware" of the 15th Georgia had been brought from the Battlefield of Gettysburg and reinterred in Laurel Grove Cemetery in Lot 853, Grave 12 on September 24, 1871. Bearden thought that the "J." could have been a misinscribed "T." (Remember, the information was originally taken from the seven-year-old inscription Robert had left on Thomas Ware's makeshift headboard and was recopied at least two more times before it appeared on the card Bearden read to me.) And the dates did not match; Ware's remains obviously were brought to Savannah singly, or, more likely, with a group shipment in 1871.

On November 25, 1989, I visited Laurel Grove Cemetery in Savannah, Georgia. Actually, there are two Laurel Grove Cemeteries, just a few blocks apart. A research assistant and I spent a good hour and a half searching a dark, forbidding cemetery filled with mosquitoes but came up empty-handed: not a single Confederate grave. Our visit to the second Laurel Grove Cemetery was slightly more productive.

There was an entire section of Confederate dead, buried chronologically as they were returned to Savannah after their deaths. There was no sign of Thomas Lewis Ware, however. Nor was there any sign of Lot 853.

However, the marked section we searched containing the Confederate known dead was Lot 864. In the center of that lot stands a monument with an inscription: "To the Confederate Dead. Here rest 'til Roll Call' The men of Gettysburg." But other graves are clustered so close to the monument that it hardly seems possible the remains of one hundred men could lie in the small area.[136]

Next to lot 864 is an unmarked area, a dozen or so feet wide and as deep as the other sections; next to that was Lot 847. Could the center section have been that set aside for the late-returning Confederate dead? Could this be Lot 853 in which Thomas Ware was buried in an unmarked and forgotten grave?

Sadly, we'll probably never know. The South after the Civil War was desperately poor. Historian and author Gregory A. Coco, who has done research on hospitals and burial sites at Gettysburg and around the South, admits that Dr. R. B. Weaver occasionally went unpaid for his efforts at disinterring the Confederate dead and returning them to the South. Though the former Rebels wanted their sons returned to the South, they barely had enough money to pay for their return and probably put off buying headstones. Years passed, and the generations who had wanted their sons' graves marked, and who knew where they had buried them, died off. Grandchildren, then great-grandchildren, with wars and dead soldiers of their own, simply forgot those Georgians buried in unmarked graves.

And Thomas Ware, soldier, writer, brother, son, and sweetheart—except for his faithfully kept, remarkably detailed dairy—has disappeared.

---

[136] Edward G. J. Richter, telephone interviews with the author, February 1992.

"*Abstract words such as glory, honor, courage, or hallow were obscene beside the concrete names of villages, the numbers of roads, the names of rivers, the numbers of regiments and the dates.*"

—Ernest Hemingway

Horner's March Route on Modern Highways

Franklin Horner and the men of the 12th Pennsylvania Reserves spent much of the time recounted in this book working on the fortifications outside of Washington, D.C. It wasn't until the Confederate Army began to enter Pennsylvania that the emergency was considered dire enough to call the troops from the defenses of Washington out into the field.

Washington, D.C., and its environs in northern Virginia have modernized so as to be virtually unrecognizable to anyone seeking a vision into the nineteenth century. While some of the places mentioned by Horner, such as Falls Church, can still be located on modern maps, others have lost their old names, and finding their modern counterparts in the maze of underpasses and traffic that is suburban Washington is not only frustrating but dangerous while traveling during rush hour.

Since the infrastructure of suburban Washington is continually changing, it is probably best to begin Franklin Horner's journey from Dranesville, Virginia, on Route 7—the June 26, 1863, entry in Horner's diary. Note that Horner is not as detailed in his descriptions of the roads he marches as Ware is. In some cases when Horner is unclear as to specific roads, the route I describe here follows the general route taken by the Union Army's Fifth Corps. I have compared modern roads with roads shown on the *Atlas to the Official Records* and have chosen the older routes.

JUNE 26, 1863. Horner marches from Balls Crossroads through Dranesville on what is now Virginia State Route 7. He probably camped near the junction of County Route 641 and Route 7, since Edwards Ferry, where the 12th Pennsylvania crossed the Potomac, is just a few miles north.

Summary. From Dranesville, Virginia, follow Route 7 northwest toward Leesburg to the junction with Route 641.

JUNE 27, 1863. Horner crossed the Potomac at Edwards Ferry. Unfortunately, the road that once led to Edwards Ferry has been obliterated by modern industrial parks and commercial buildings, so you must continue along Route 7 to U.S. Route 15 north at Leesburg. The shortest route to the Maryland side of the Potomac is via a quaint ferry system at Whites Ferry. Just after the Route 15–Leesburg bypass ends, follow 15 north to county road 655 and turn right. The road will dead-end at Whites Ferry. The ferry runs all year round from 6:00 A.M. to 11:00 P.M. except when there is floating ice or debris in the Potomac. You may have to wait a few minutes for the ferry to recross the Potomac. The charge for cars to cross, the last time I checked, was $2.25.

After crossing the Potomac, turn right onto River Road, a dirt and gravel road that leads to Edwards Ferry. It is unlikely that Franklin Horner and his unit used this road, which follows the wide curve of the Potomac, since it would have taken them the long route to their campsite. But for its entire length, the road looks as it must have during the nineteenth century—exactly as the other roads used by Horner and the two armies approaching each other probably appeared as they tramped them during the Gettysburg Campaign. Go slowly and watch for the signs to stay on River Road.

River Road dead-ends into Edwards Ferry Road at the ferry site, now a part of the Chesapeake and Ohio Canal National Park. Turn right and follow the road across the C&O Canal and down to the Potomac where the pontoon bridges were laid for Horner and his unit to cross.

Leaving Edwards Ferry, follow Edwards Ferry Road. Be careful to stay on Edwards Ferry Road, particularly where Westerley Road branches to the right and Edwards Ferry Road bears left. Whites Ferry Road crosses Edwards Ferry Road; continue straight on Edwards Ferry Road until it becomes Wasche Road. Turn right where Wasche Road strikes Martinsburg Road.

Where Martinsburg Road intersects Darnestown Road (Route 28), turn left onto Dickerson Road. Go under the railroad underpass and bear left at the stop sign. At the next crossroads, turn left onto Mouth of the Monocacy Road. Nearing the end of Mouth of the Monocacy Road, there is a fork; bear left at the sign to the aqueduct. Park your car and explore the area used by Horner and the Union troops for their campsite.

Summary. Go northwest on Route 7 to U.S. 15 north. Turn right onto 655 and follow to Whites Ferry. Cross the Potomac on the ferry and turn right onto River Road. Follow River Road to Edwards Ferry Road and turn right to see Edwards Ferry Potomac crossing. From Edwards Ferry take Edwards Ferry Road (which becomes Wasche Road) to Martinsburg Road and turn right; follow to Darnestown Road and turn left onto Route 28 (Dickerson Road). Go under the railroad underpass and turn left at the stop sign. At the next crossroads, turn left onto Mouth of the Monocacy Road; bear left toward aqueduct and park in lot.

JUNE 28, 1863. Horner's unit marched from the Mouth of the Monocacy through what he calls Buckstown. Buckeystown, Maryland, is on State Route 85. The Union Army's Fifth Corps, on June 28, 1863, was located just south of Frederick, Maryland. Horner's unit merged with the Fifth Corps and camped with them near Frederick.

Summary. Follow Mouth of the Monocacy Road from the parking lot to the main road, which is Route 28. Turn left and follow 28 west to Route 85. Follow 85 north through Buckeystown and to Frederick.

JUNE 29, 1863. Horner says that they marched past Frederick City. It is impossible to know his exact route since construction around Frederick has altered much, but we do know that he ended up near Liberty, Maryland. There is a Libertytown on Route 26 along the way to Uniontown, where he encamped June 30. Assuming Libertytown was once Liberty (or that Horner abbreviated the name or heard it wrong), it is best to follow Route 85 north to U.S. 15 north, a bypass around Frederick. From Route 15, exit onto Route 26 and follow it east to Libertytown.

Summary. Take Route 85 north to U.S. 15 north bypass around Frederick. Exit onto Route 26 east and follow to Libertytown.

JUNE 30, 1863. Horner's diary entry details the towns he goes through but not the routes he takes. While there are a number of smaller secondary roads through this section of Maryland, it is impossible to know if Horner took those—or even if they existed—during the campaign in 1863. The exact routes across these few miles are not all that important; the general flavor and feeling of the landscape and terrain are everywhere in this section of Maryland, with its rolling hills and farm fields. We know from Horner's entries that he passed through Liberty (Libertytown), Union Bridge, and Muttontown (a name that has disappeared even from detailed county maps), and camped near Uniontown. Following Route 75 north from Libertytown takes you through Johnsville and Union Bridge, and eventually to Route 84. Follow 84 north to Uniontown.

Summary. Follow Route 26 into Libertytown. Take Route 75 north to Union Bridge, then Route 84 north to Uniontown.

JULY 1, 1863. Horner doesn't mention his route from Uniontown, but we know from the records of the march that they ended up near Hanover, Pennsylvania (in, as Horner mentions, York County). The roads between Uniontown and Hanover are a maze, some perhaps historic, many not. The best route to take to Hanover using some of the older roads is to follow Uniontown Road east to Westminster. To avoid going through Westminster, turn left at the first light, several miles out of Uniontown, which is Maryland Route 31 east, or the Westminster bypass. Then take Route 140 east to Route 97 north toward Gettysburg.

A few miles north on 97 you will pass through Union Mills, a restored settlement where Confederate general Jeb Stuart spent the night on June 29, 1863, and where Union general James Barnes spent the next night.

Continuing north on 97, turn right onto Cherrytown Road in Silver Run. According to other unpublished diaries, at least a part of the Union Army's Fifth Corps passed along Cherrytown Road. At the stop sign, turn left onto Old Hanover Road. Just past the Pennsylvania state line, be careful to bear right onto Old Westminster Road.

At the next stop sign, turn left onto what is marked Granite

Valley Road. It is Old Westminster Road and will dead-end into Pennsylvania Route 194. At 194 turn right. You'll see a sign describing the cavalry battle between Union general Judson Kilpatrick's cavalry and Jeb Stuart's Confederate Cavalry in Hanover. (Horner's unit was not the first to pass this way. Nearly every road within fifty miles of Gettysburg was covered at one time or another by the cavalry.) Follow 194 north to Route 116 west. Turn left and follow 116 through the outskirts of Hanover to McSherrystown, where Horner and the men of the Fifth Corps camped.

Summary. From Uniontown, take Uniontown Road to the first stoplight; turn left onto Maryland Route 31 east. Then follow Route 140 east to Route 97 north toward Gettysburg. Follow 97 north to Silver Run, then turn right onto Cherrytown Road. At the stop sign, turn left onto Old Hanover Road. Follow Old Hanover Road as it crosses the Pennsylvania state line, then bear right onto Old Westminster Road. Turn left onto Granite Valley Road (which is still Old Westminster Road) and follow straight until it dead-ends at Route 194. Turn right and follow 194 north to Route 116 west. Turn left onto 116 west and follow it to McSherrystown.

JULY 2, 1863. Route 116 west was the main road from McSherrystown to Gettysburg. By the time Horner and the men of the 12th Pennsylvania were approaching Gettysburg, however, Confederates were already occupying it. Union troops coming in from this direction had to veer off to the southwest to approach the Union lines from behind. Follow Route 116 through Bonneauville about one and one-half miles to Low Dutch Road and take a left; this puts you on one of the most traveled roads to the rear of the Union Army.

Low Dutch Road dead-ends into Baltimore Road, and a right turn will head you to the rear of what were once the Union lines at Gettysburg. Passing over Rock Creek, you will see on the left the entrance to Gettysburg National Military Park. This is the most direct route to where Horner's unit ended up on the battlefield. Turn left at the sign, but go straight at the next sign to the park onto Blacksmith Shop Road. At the stop sign, turn right, remaining on Blacksmith Shop Road. As you approach the end of the road, you will begin to see the back of Little Round Top to your left. A left at the stop sign (Taneytown Road) and an immediate right onto Wheatfield Road will take you up the northern slope of Little Round Top. To the right in this general area and up over the small ridge was where units, including Horner's, were held in preparation to go into the battle. Rereading Crawford's Report in the July 2, 1863, section will help orient you to their position vis-à-vis the ground you are traveling across.

Continue past the stop sign and down into the valley. On the right is where Crawford's Division was massed prior to moving into battle. Turn left onto the next road, Crawford Avenue. To the left on the slope of Little Round Top is where Crawford states that Fisher's Brigade, including the 12th Pennsylvania and the rest of Crawford's Division, was ordered.

At the next stop sign turn left. The group of large boulders to your right rear is Devil's Den, and just beyond is the Triangular Field where Thomas Ware was fighting. On the right is the north slope of Big Round Top, where, within 150 yards, Franklin Horner's unit was detached. Nearing the top of the hill, park at the area on the right and walk to the right along Sykes Avenue (at the stop sign) to the monument to Fisher's Brigade on the left. It was in this area that Horner fought during the battle.

Summary. Follow Route 116 west from McSherrystown to Low Dutch Road; left on Low Dutch Road to Baltimore Road, where you turn right. Cross Rock Creek and turn left at the Gettysburg National Park entrance sign. Bear left onto Blacksmith Shop Road and follow to Taneytown Road. Take a left and then an immediate right onto Wheatfield Road. At Crawford Avenue, take a left and follow to stop sign at Warren Avenue; turn left on Warren Avenue to parking area.

Ware's March Route on Modern Highways

Most of the route of Thomas Ware from Culpeper, Virginia, to the Triangular Field in Gettysburg, Pennsylvania, can be followed by automobile today. While we cannot be perfectly precise as to the routes Ware took, common sense tells us that the soldiers would have taken the most direct route, except in some notable cases when other marching units had priority. Occasionally several roads lead around hills and mountains to the place Ware mentions. In reconstructing his route, I have used the modern roads that also appear on Civil War maps to ensure I've chosen the oldest roads in the area.

Some of the roads are back roads not particularly suited for modern vehicular traffic, and I don't recommend that you take off across private land where Ware and the men of the 15th Georgia did. Walking along the roadside ascending the mountains into Ashby's or Snicker's Gap, however, or marching the long, hilly road from Delaplane to Upperville might lend some insight into what Ware and his fellow soldiers in the Confederate Army endured during the Gettysburg Campaign. Of course, a visit to the Triangular Field is a must.

Ware began his actual journey north from Cedar Run on June 15, 1863; his movements around Culpeper, including his marches to Pony Mountain, Brandy Station, and Cedar Run are not included in this appendix because they are not a part of the invasion route. These side trips can be reconstructed using Ware's descriptions within the text, however. To begin Ware's march on the Gettysburg Campaign, begin in Culpeper and find Virginia State Route 229 north off U.S. Routes 15 and 29.

JUNE 15, 1863. From Culpeper, both modern Routes 522 and 729 lead to Front Royal and Winchester. Measurement of the two from Culpeper to where Ware camped just beyond the Thornton River, as well as Ware's statement that they marched one and one-half miles beyond the town to begin their march from Culpeper, indicates that Ware and the men of the 15th Georgia probably took Route 729 for about nine miles (as he states) until they crossed the Hazel River. Route 729 continues into Rappahannock County. Almost exactly eighteen miles from their original campsite of June 14–15 near Cedar Run south of Culpeper, they encamped somewhere just beyond the river, probably near it so as to be close to water.

Summary. From Culpeper, take Virginia State Route 229 north one and one-half miles to 729 to beyond the Thornton River.

JUNE 16, 1863. Ware's unit probably followed modern Route 729 until they struck modern Route 647 at Flint Hill. Ware calls this area "'Hains' X roads" but the *Atlas to the Official Records* calls it "Gaines Crossroads." The men of the 15th Georgia left Route 647 and cut across "plantations" until they hit modern Route 688, the road to Markham. Somewhere along 688 they passed through what is identified on old maps as "Barbee's Cross-roads," which Ware calls "Darby's X roads." They camped at Markham.

Summary. Follow Route 729 to Flint Hill; then take Route 647 east to Route 688; turn left on 688 north to Markham.

JUNE 17, 1863. According to Ware, the Confederates marched along the railroad for some time. If you are driving, follow Route 55 east to Route 17 north and turn left toward Delaplane. After crossing the railroad tracks, turn right into Delaplane. Here, as Ware describes it, was where Gen. Joseph E. Johnston loaded his troops onto trains for the Battle of Manassas, the first time in military history that railroads were used for transporting troops to battle. From Delaplane, take Route 712 north and follow the road Ware describes as having very long hills and numerous rock fences. You'll pass the same church Ware passed on the outskirts of Upperville. Turn right where 712 dead-ends into Route 50, and go east about a mile and a half to where Ware and the 15th Georgia encamped for the night.

Summary. From Markham take Route 55 east to Route 17;

turn left onto Route 17 north and follow to Delaplane. Cross the railroad tracks and turn right. Take Route 712 to Upperville. Turn right on Route 50 east, and go one and one-half miles to Ware's campsite.

JUNE 18, 1863. From Ware's campsite one and one-half miles east of Upperville, turn around and drive back through Upperville on Route 50. Follow 50 west through Ashby's Gap. (A nice side trip is through the small village of Paris, which is the route of the old road through Ashby's Gap.) Continue west on Route 50 (which has joined with Route 17) until you cross the Shenandoah River. If you care to see the limestone spring Ware talks about, take the first right once over the bridge and follow it under the bridge. To the right you'll see the stream from the spring, and the modern springhouse can be seen when there are no leaves on the trees. It is on private property. A mile from the river, on modern Route 50/17 near the junction with Route 723, Ware camped for the night.

Summary. Travel west on Route 50 through Ashby's Gap; cross the Shenandoah River and drive one mile to Ware's campsite at or near where Route 723 bears right from Route 50/17. (Note side trips described above.)

JUNE 19, 1863. Near where Ware camped on the night of June 18–19, Route 723 forks to the northwest from Route 50. Route 723 is the only way you can get from Route 50 to Route 621, the likely road Ware took along the Shenandoah River to Snicker's Gap on Route 7. Some of the river road Ware walked along has changed since the 1860s, but much of it has stayed exactly the way it was when Ware tramped his way along the Shenandoah: winding, dirt- and gravel-covered, undulating with the route of the river. Route 621 angles away from the river until it strikes Route 7, where you must turn right to cross the Shenandoah. Ware crossed the river near where the bridge for modern Route 7 crosses it. After a long uphill march, Ware camped for the night three hundred yards up the east slope of the mountain on Route 7, the Leesburg Pike.

Summary. Take Route 723 northwest off of Route 50. Then take Route 621 north along the river to Route 7. Turn right, cross the river, and follow Route 7 east through Snicker's Gap to Ware's campsite.

JUNE 20, 1863. Ware and the men of the 15th Georgia marched back up the mountain about a mile, built breastworks of rock three feet high, and were ordered through the gap and across the river again. About a mile across the river, they encamped in a grove near Route 7 where they spent the night and the next day.

Summary. Return along Route 7 west through Snicker's Gap, cross the river, and continue about a mile to Ware's campsite of June 20–21.

JUNE 21, 1863. No movement.

JUNE 22, 1863. Ware returned from his camp about a mile from the river along the same route he marched on June 19. Probably at Route 723 his unit turned right, since this is the shortest route to Millwood (although military logic, as we have seen, doesn't always find that a straight line is the shortest distance between two points). They camped somewhere in the vicinity of the historic town of Millwood.

Summary. Return to Route 621 and follow it south along the river to Route 723. Turn right and follow 723 west to Millwood.

JUNE 23, 1863. No movement.

JUNE 24, 1863. The march north from Millwood to Berryville took Ware along modern Route 255, which turns into U.S. Route 340 two miles north of Millwood. Since Ware mentions marching through "Summer Point" (Summit Point on modern maps), the 15th Georgia must have gotten onto modern Jefferson County Route 1 via a left turn onto Route 611 north about a mile and a half north of Berryville. After they passed through Summit Point, they crossed fields to get to Middleway. The easiest way to get there by car is to continue to follow Route 1. They then crossed Opequon Creek and followed the Bunker Hill Turnpike. As of this writing, the older road—1/8—which leads to the crossing of the Opequon, is closed. But by following Route 1 north through Middleway and turning left onto Route 51 west, you can cross the Opequon less than a mile from where Ware did. Cross the river into Berkeley County, turn left at the first crossroads (Route 51/9, "Three Run

Road") and turn right at the stop sign onto Route 26. You will pass a mill and a farmhouse, which may very well be where Ware and the men of the 15th camped the night of June 24, 1863.

Summary. From Millwood, head north on Route 255, which becomes Route 340. Continue to Route 611 north and take a left. Follow 611 into West Virginia, where it becomes Route 1. Follow this to Middleway. Continue through Middleway and make a left onto Route 51 west. Turn left onto 51/9, then right onto Route 26. Follow this road about two miles to Ware's campsite.

JUNE 25, 1863. Ware's description is a little confusing in that he doesn't mention being in Berkeley County until he's nearly at Martinsburg. Either he didn't see a sign at Opequon Creek, or the county lines have changed since Ware passed that way. Nevertheless, he probably marched Route 26 from the unit's campsite to what he calls "country roads" that bypass Bunker Hill. Any small "country roads" running parallel to modern U.S. Route 11 seem to have disappeared, perhaps obliterated by disuse and the passing of time. Following Route 11, however, will give a general idea of the terrain and vistas Ware experienced. Route 26 eventually intersects Route 11, where turning right heads you northward. Ware skirted the town of Martinsburg and marched another six miles to their campsite, probably near where the Potomac River approaches Route 11. Following Route 11 through Martinsburg is simple, and the route is well marked.

Summary. Continue along Route 26 to U.S. 11 north. Follow Route 11 six miles north of Martinsburg, West Virginia, to Ware's campsite.

JUNE 26, 1863. Four more miles on U.S. Route 11 takes you to the Potomac River. From the modern bridge you can see the aqueduct of the Chesapeake and Ohio Canal on the left. (It is a nice side trip down to the historic canal.) The shallows of the river where the men waded across are sometimes visible to the right of the bridge during low water. The 15th Georgia continued to march Route 11 through Williamsport, then cut across a country road to the road to Greencastle, Pennsylvania (Maryland State Route 63), where it approaches the Conococheague Creek. Just over the Pennsylvania state line, they encamped.

Summary. Continue north on Route 11, across the Potomac River to Williamsport where you make a left onto Route 63 north. Continue north to the Pennsylvania line.

JUNE 27, 1863. Route 63 turns into U.S. 11 about four miles or so from Ware's campsite just south of Greencastle, Pennsylvania. Follow Route 11 through Greencastle another eleven miles to Chambersburg. Ware doesn't say which way he went after they marched three miles beyond Chambersburg and left the turnpike, but somewhere north of the small town, the men of the 15th Georgia and the rest of Benning's Brigade encamped.

Summary. Continue north on Route 63 to Route 11. Follow 11 through Greencastle to Chambersburg; three miles north of Chambersburg is Ware's campground.

JUNE 28, 1863. No movement.

JUNE 29, 1863. Ware doesn't detail the exact route his regiment, along with the 17th Georgia and others, took to tear up the railroad. Perhaps they marched along the railroad as they tore it up, or perhaps they marched on the roads to Scotland and began destroying the railroad as they worked their way back toward the other units. Just a few miles north of Ware's campsite (actually about 4.8 miles north of Chambersburg), Route 11 intersects Route 997. (It is marked with an arrow to Scotland, signifying it as a truck route.) Turn right on 997 south. After about a mile, the road forks. The right fork will take you to the site of the railroad bridge Ware and the 15th Georgia burned, now replaced with a concrete bridge. Near the bridge to the left of the road are some Civil War–era buildings, one of which may have been the location of the depot Ware mentions as being spared from destruction.

Summary. Take Route 11 north to Route 997 south and turn right. At the fork, bear right to Scotland railroad bridge.

JUNE 30, 1863. Ware states that they marched slowly on a very crooked road until they reached Fayetteville, Pennsylvania.

The road through Scotland has a branch to the right in the town that eventually reaches U.S. Route 30 at Fayetteville. After the railroad bridge, take the second right, marked Woodstock Road (State Route 1003), and follow to U.S. Route 30.

Summary. Continuing from the Scotland railroad bridge, take the second right, onto Route 1003 (Woodstock Road). Follow this to U.S. Route 30 east. Turn left and follow to the sign for Fayetteville; make a left into Fayetteville.

JULY 1, 1863. Ware and the men of the brigade marched through the small village of Fayetteville. The road through Fayetteville eventually reintersects Route 30. Follow Route 30 east for about five miles until you see a sign for Route 234. Turn right at this sign. Note that you will not be traveling on Route 234 (which goes only to the left), but on a small road that parallels modern Route 30 east and represents what is left of old Route 30. This is the route that the Confederate Army took to Gettysburg. About three and a half miles from where you enter old Route 30, you will pass on the left the Cashtown Inn, where numerous southern officers stopped for refreshment and information on their way to Gettysburg. Continue following old Route 30 (Route 234) through McKnightstown until it rejoins modern Route 30, then follow modern Route 30 toward Gettysburg about four miles, to where the men of the 15th Georgia encamped outside the town—somewhere between where Willoughby Run crosses Route 30 and where the Lutheran seminary still stands.

Summary. Go through Fayetteville and out onto Route 30. Take Route 30 to the sign for Route 234 and turn right onto old Route 30. Follow this through Cashtown and McKnightstown, then out onto Route 30 again. Continue about four miles to the Lutheran seminary on the outskirts of Gettysburg.

JULY 2, 1863. Ware and the men of the 15th Georgia began a strange loop back toward Chambersburg, a left turn southward toward Black Horse Tavern on the Fairfield Road, then a return to follow the western slope of Seminary Ridge. (The route can be partially reconstructed by the careful historian but can barely be traveled in its entirety by car.) Turn right at the Lutheran seminary and follow Seminary Ridge southward to approximate Ware's march on July 2 and end up where his attack began.

Follow West Confederate Avenue southward past the Lutheran seminary, through the traffic light, and along the Confederate battle lines. The valley to the right, sheltered from the Union signalmen on Little Round Top, provided the perfect staging and movement area for the Confederates. Cross Wheatfield Road at the first stop sign, then cross Route 15—Emmitsburg Road—at the second stop sign, and you will be in the area where the men of Benning's Brigade formed for their assault in the late afternoon of July 2, 1863. They marched down the slopes to your left, into the woods, and closed in on the triangular field. Note the M. Bushman farm on the left.

Continue to follow West Confederate Avenue until you reach the next stop sign; turn left, descending into the valley of Devil's Den. (Just before the stop sign, on the right, you will have passed the monument to Franklin Horner's brigade.) At the stop sign, turn left again, and follow the winding road around the massive boulders until you see Smith's Battery on the right. Park just beyond it. Cross the road to the gated rail fence. This is the Triangular Field where Ware fought.

Summary. At the Lutheran seminary, turn right off Route 30 onto West Confederate Avenue. Follow West Confederate Avenue past one stop light to the third stop sign and turn left. Make another left at the next stop sign to Smith's Battery above Devil's Den; cross the road to the Triangular Field.

"Because no battle is ever won he said. They are not even fought. The field only reveals to man his own folly and despair, and victory is an illusion of philosophers and fools."

—William Faulkner

The Effects of Casualties under the Civil War System of Recruiting

S omeone once, in analyzing military combat units, came up with the figure of 15 percent as the maximum amount of casualties a military unit could sustain before ceasing to be combat effective. William Manchester, in his classic *Goodbye, Darkness*, says that it is "a military maxim, repeated down the ages, that casualties of 30 percent are usually the most a fighting unit can endure without losing combative spirit."[137] Both of these figures seem too low when viewed in the light of all of military history, considering how many units have suffered 50, 60, and even 80 percent casualties and still could claim victory at the end of the battle.

But victory on the battlefield in spite of high losses certainly doesn't tell the whole story.

During the Civil War, when recruiting was done on a parochial level, it was not cold, faceless, numbered combat units that were decimated by the losses. When casualty lists arrived in the small towns of the North and the South, they revealed that entire families had been destroyed.

Exact figures and percentages of losses are difficult, if not impossible, to come by. For the following analysis I used the *Official Records*, Samuel P. Bates's *History of Pennsylvania Volunteers*, Volume 1, and Lillian Henderson's *Roster of the Confederate Soldiers from Georgia, 1861-1865*, as well as figures from John W. Busey and David G. Martin's *Regimental Strengths at Gettysburg* and Edward G. J. Richter. Bates and Henderson are most important because they name individuals rather than merely listing numbers. Numbers do not fight battles, people with first names and last names do. Numbers do not trade life for ground, fathers and brothers and sons do.

---

[137] Manchester, 255.

Franklin Horner's regiment, the 12th Pennsylvania Reserves, entered the Battle of Gettysburg with 320 men on its roster. It is estimated that only 272 of them were actually engaged in any kind of marching or fighting on the battlefield.[138] Of those, one man was wounded and one was killed, a percentage of loss of about .7 percent.

An analysis of Horner's Company H, recruited in Indiana County, Pennsylvania, shows that 117 men were assigned to the company over the course of the war. Forty-three of them became casualties—about 36.7 percent.[139]

But mere numbers do not tell all. The family name Altimus appears twice in the roster for Company H, 12th Pennsylvania Reserves. Possibly the two were cousins. William was discharged for wounds received at Mechanicsville, June 27, 1862, and William W. was discharged after being wounded at South Mountain, September 14, 1862.

Two Brackens show up on the company roster. One was discharged on a surgeon's certificate, obviously taken ill by the rigors of soldiering.

Sergeant Dick, whom Horner refers to as leaving for recruiting duty, returned to the company only to be wounded on May 8, 1864. Pvt. George W. Dick, possibly a younger relative, died of wounds received at Fredericksburg, Virginia.

The Overdorff family was particularly hard hit: Francis was discharged on a surgeon's certificate; Harvey was killed at Charles City Cross Roads on June 30, 1862; and David was killed at Antietam on September 17, 1862.[140]

Thomas Ware's regiment, the 15th Georgia, took between 330 and 335 men into the Battle of Gettysburg, according to Colonel Du Bose.[141] Most accounts agree approximately with Du Bose's figure of 171 casualties for the battle. Using Du Bose's estimated troop strength of 330 to 335, the casualties for the 15th Georgia during the Battle of Gettysburg were 51 to 52 percent.

---

[138] Busey and Martin, 66.

[139] Bates, Vol. 1, 901-2.

[140] Ibid.

[141] *O.R.*, Vol. 27, part 2, 424. Busey and Martin's analysis of the June 30, 1863, roster places the regimental strength at 387 and estimates 368 of them were engaged.

A total of 115 men were recruited from Lincoln County, Georgia, from 1861 to 1865 for Ware's Company G. Seventy-nine men became casualties during the war, for a casualty percentage of 68.7 percent: 39 were killed in battle or died of other causes, 16 were wounded, 12 were listed as missing, and 12 were disabled from their service.[142]

The casualty lists for Company G, 15th Georgia Infantry reveal the truly personal tragedy of the American Civil War. In just three years and nine months, vital, animate families were cut to pieces as they lost their brothers and cousins, fathers and husbands and sons, who had happily rushed to the colors along with Thomas Ware on July 15, 1861.[143]

The Caver family put two men into the service. Both were wounded and one died.

The Clary family gave up three men and saw two return wounded.

The Colvins sent two. One was wounded and subsequently died.

The Crawfords sent four. One died and another was wounded.

The Florences gave up three, only to see one wounded and the other two come home in coffins.

The Fergersons sent two. One died.

The Leverett family put four boys in uniform. One died in service, one was killed in battle, and one was captured.

The Normans gave up three to the cause. Of those, George, wounded at Antietam, returned to be captured at Gettysburg, and Peyton, who had suffered a skull fracture at Second Manassas, was also captured at Gettysburg.

The Sale family lost one killed of two boys sent.

The Remsen family saw two wounded of three who enlisted.

The Parks family sent two. One was wounded and died.

The Cullars sent two. One was captured.

The Cartledges sent three. One was wounded and died.

Nicholas and Matilda Ware saw three of their boys go off to war and felt the pain of having their first-born killed and their next oldest remain a prisoner of war for nineteen months.

---

[142] Henderson, 454-60.
[143] Ibid.

Perhaps the saddest of all were the Gullatt, Jones, and Cauley families.

The Gullatts lost three out of four sons sent to war. Henderson died in camp near Orange Court House, Virginia, on April 6, 1862. Just four months later, on August 30, 1862, Peter was killed at Second Manassas. Absalom died of pneumonia in Richmond on May 28, 1864, and lies buried there in Hollywood Cemetery, far from Lincoln County, Georgia.

The Jones family lost both their sons: Moses died of typhoid fever less than two months after enlisting; Joshua was discharged as disabled in 1861 but reenlisted, only to be killed at Gettysburg on July 2, 1863.

The Cauleys lost all three of the sons they sent. Luke's records are muddled, but he was captured at Gettysburg and appears to have died in a hospital at Point Lookout, Maryland, on January 12, 1864, after three months of chronic diarrhea. And on May 10, 1864, at Spotsylvania, Virginia, both Clem and Henry Cauley were slain in battle, probably within a few horrifying minutes of one another.

If you wanted to find the glory in war that had been predicted from podiums and pulpits just four short years before, neither Indiana County, Pennsylvania, nor Lincoln County, Georgia, was the place to seek it in 1865.

Bibliography

Bates, Samuel P. *The History of Pennsylvania Volunteers, 1861–1865.*
5 Volumes. Harrisburg, PA: B. Singerly, State Printer, 1869–1871.

Billings, John D. *Hardtack and Coffee or The Unwritten Story of Army
Life.* Boston: George M. Smith & Co., 1889; reprinted. Gettysburg, PA: Civil War Times Illustrated, 1974.

Busey, John W., and David G. Martin. *Regimental Strengths and
Losses at Gettysburg.* Hightstown, NJ: Longstreet House, 1986.

Chamberlain, Joshua L. *The Passing of the Armies.* Dayton, OH:
Morningside Bookshop, 1982.

Coddington, Edwin B. *The Gettysburg Campaign: A Study in Command.*
New York: Charles Scribner's Sons, 1968.

Cowles, Capt. Calvin D., compiler. *Atlas to Accompany the Official
Records of the Union and Confederate Armies.* Washington, DC:
Government Printing Office, 1891–95.

Culpeper Historical Society. *Historic Culpeper.* Culpeper, VA:
Culpeper Historical Society, 1974.

Davis, Burke. *Jeb Stuart: The Last Cavalier.* New York: The Fairfax
Press, 1988.

Dyer, Gwynne. *War.* New York: Crown Publishers, 1985.

Freeman, Douglas S. *Lee's Lieutenants.* New York: Charles Scribner's
Sons, 1946.

Fremantle, Lt. Col. Arthur. *Three Months in the Southern States.*
London: William Blackwood and Sons, 1863.

Gaff, Alan D. *Brave Men's Tears: The Iron Brigade at Brawner Farm.*
Dayton, OH: Morningside Bookshop, 1985.

Gallant, T. Grady. *The Friendly Dead.* Garden City, NJ: Doubleday,
1964.

Galwey, Thomas F. *The Valiant Hours.* Edited by W. S. Nye. Harrisburg, PA: Stackpole Books, 1961.

Georgia Department of Archives and History, Atlanta, GA. Service Records of Civil War Soldiers: Thomas Ware Files; Robert Ware Files.

Georgia Historical Society, Savannah, GA. Burial Records of Laurel Grove Cemetery, Savannah, GA, per researchers Tracy Bearden and Karen E. Osvald.

Gettysburg National Military Park Vertical Files, Gettysburg, PA. Savannah, Georgia, Ladies Memorial Association file.

Guinn, J. Russell. Interview with the author, 1990.

Hahn, Thomas F. *Towpath Guide to the C&O Canal.* Shepherdstown, WV: The American Canal & Transportation Center, 1983.

Harrison, Kathleen R. Georg. "Our Principle Loss Was in This Place." *Gettysburg: Historical Articles of Lasting Interest.* July 1989.

Henderson, Lillian. *Roster of the Confederate Soldiers of Georgia, 1861–1865.* Compiled for the State of Georgia, 1960.

Holmes, Richard. *Acts of War: The Behavior of Men in Battle.* New York: Free Press, 1986.

Horan, James D. *Timothy O'Sullivan: America's Forgotten Photographer.* New York: Bonanza Books, 1966.

Horner, Franklin. Unpublished diaries, Gettysburg National Military Park Curatorial Collection, Gettysburg, PA.

Johnson, Otto, ed. *Information Please Almanac, Atlas & Yearbook 1987.* Boston: Houghton, Mifflin Co., 1987.

Livermore, Thomas L. *Numbers and Losses in the Civil War.* Boston: Houghton, Mifflin & Co., 1900.

Long, E.B., and Barbara Long. *The Civil War Day by Day: An Almanac.* Garden City, NJ: Doubleday & Co. Inc., 1971.

Manchester, William. *Goodbye, Darkness.* Boston: Little, Brown & Co., 1979.

McCarthy, Carlton. *Detailed Minutiae of Soldier Life in the Army of Northern Virginia.* Richmond, VA: Carlton McCarthy and Company, 1882. Reprint. Alexandria, VA: Time-Life Books, Inc., 1981.

Martin, Rosemarie. Interviews with the author, 1990.

Murfin, James V. *The Gleam of Bayonets: The Battle of Antietam and the Maryland Campaign of 1862.* New York: Thomas Yoseloff, 1965.

National Archives Military Service Records, Franklin Horner Files. National Archives, Washington, DC.

Nesbitt, Mark. *If the South Won Gettysburg.* Gettysburg, PA: Reliance Publishing Co., 1980.

Norman, Kenneth. Personal files. Collection of correspondence and research on the Norman and Ware families. Obtained through correspondence and interviews with the author, 1990–91.

Official Records of the War of the Rebellion: Series I, vol. 27, parts 1, 2, 3. Washington, DC: Government Printing Office, 1889.

Parsons, H. C. "Farnsworth's Charge and Death." In *Battles and Leaders of the Civil War,* Vol. 3. Edited by Robert Underwood Johnson and Clarence Clough Buel. *Century Magazine,* 1889; reprint ed., Secaucus, NJ: Castle.

Probst, Mary. Personal files. Collection of correspondence and research on her grandfather, Robert Ware, and his brother, Thomas. Obtained through correspondence and interviews, 1989–91.

Richter, Edward G. J. "The Removal of the Confederate Dead from Gettysburg." *Gettysburg: Historical Articles of Lasting Interest,* January 1990, 113.

———. Telephone interviews with the author. February 25–26, 1992.

Schildt, John W. *Stonewall Jackson: Day by Day.* Chewsville, MD: Antietam Publications, Undated (c. 1985).

Sledge, E. B. *With the Old Breed at Peleliu and Okinawa.* Novato, CA: Presidio Press, 1981.

Storrick, William C. "Battlefield Notes—Story of Joseph Wasden." Gettysburg, PA: *Gettysburg Compiler,* July 24, 1926.

Thomason, John W., Jr. *Jeb Stuart.* New York: Charles Scribner's Sons, 1930.

Tilberg, Dr. Frederick. *Vignettes of the Battlefield.* Unpublished paper, Gettysburg National Military Park Files.

Todd, Frederick P. *American Military Equipage: 1851–1872.* New York: Charles Scribner's Sons, 1978.

Tucker, Glenn. *High Tide at Gettysburg: The Campaign in Pennsylvania.* Indianapolis: The Bobbs-Merrill Co., Inc., 1958.

———. *Lee and Longstreet at Gettysburg.* Indianapolis: The Bobbs-Merrill Co., Inc., 1968.

Ware, Thomas Lewis. Unpublished diaries. Southern Historical Collection, University of North Carolina, Chapel Hill.

Wiley, Bell I. *The Life of Billy Yank: The Common Soldier of the Union.* Indianapolis: The Bobbs-Merrill Co., Inc., 1952.

————. *The Life of Johnny Reb: The Common Soldier of the Confederacy.* Indianapolis: The Bobbs-Merrill Co., Inc., 1962 (Charter Edition).

Index